Writing Forms

Tops and Bottoms

Storybook Characters

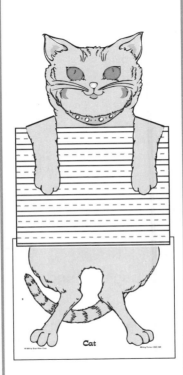

Cat

pages 2–42

Holidays

Easter Bunny

pages 43–86

Children Around the World

An Inuit Girl

pages 87–132

People at Work

Bus Driver

pages 133–160

Four Kinds of Writing Forms

- Add pizzazz to student writing assignments.
- Just add your own writing paper.
- Enrich language arts and social studies.

D1560977

Author: Jo Ellen Moore
Editor: Marilyn Evans
Illustrator: Jo Larsen
Designer: Jo Larsen
Desktop: Jo Larsen
Cover design: Cheryl Puckett

Entire contents ©1999 by EVAN-MOOR CORP.
18 Lower Ragsdale Drive, Monterey, CA 93940-5746.
Permission is hereby granted to the individual purchaser to reproduce student materials in this book for noncommercial individual or classroom use only. Permission is not granted for schoolwide, or systemwide, reproduction of materials.
Printed in U.S.A.

EMC 596

Storybook Characters Writing Forms

Storybook Characters writing forms can be used to:

- retell favorite parts of the story
- write a review of the story
- outline the plot
- write new adventures about a character
- write a poem about a character
- invent new stories
- practice handwriting
- list books read about similar characters
- hold student work on a bulletin board display

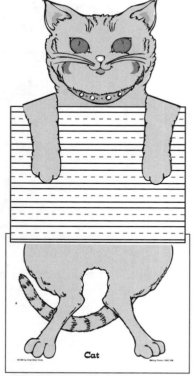

Cut out the "top."

Paste your own paper to the "top."

Paste the "bottom" to your paper.

Cat

Monkey ▪▪▪▪▪▪▪▪▪▪▪▪▪▪▪▪▪▪▪▪▪▪▪▪▪▪▪▪▪▪▪ **pages 7 and 8**

Use the **monkey** writing form with books such as:

Caps for Sale by Esphyr Slodbokina; HarperCollins Juvenile Books, 1988.
Curious George Goes to School by Margaret Rey, H. A. Rey, and Allan J. Shalleck; Houghton Mifflin Company, 1989.
Curious George Rides a Bike by H. A. Rey; Houghton Mifflin, 1973.
Monkey Do! by Allan Ahlberg and Andre Amustz; Candlewick Press, 1998.
Pedro and the Monkey by Robert D. San Souci; William Morris and Company, 1996.

Pig ▪▪▪▪▪▪▪▪▪▪▪▪▪▪▪▪▪▪▪▪▪▪▪▪▪▪▪▪▪▪▪▪▪▪ **pages 9 and 10**

Use the **pig** writing form with books such as:

All Pigs Are Beautiful by Dick King-Smith; Candlewick Press, 1993.
Five Little Piggies by David Martin; Candlewick Press, 1998.
The Three Little Pigs by Steven Kellogg; William Morrow and Company, 1997.
The Three Little Wolves and the Big Bad Pig by Eugene Trivizas; Aladdin Paperbacks, 1997.
A Treeful of Pigs by Arnold Lobel; Greenwillow, 1987.

Turtle • **pages 11 and 12**

Use the **turtle** writing form with books such as:

And Still the Turtle Watched by Sheila MacGill-Callahan; Puffin, 1996.
Eleven Turtle Tales: Adventure Tales from Around the World by Pleasant
 Despain; August House Publications, 1994.
Shy Little Turtle by Howard Goldsmith; McGraw-Hill, 1997.
The Tortoise and the Hare: An Aesop Fable by Janet Stevens; Holiday
 House, 1985.
The Turtle and the Moon by Charles Turner; E. P. Dutton, 1991.

Frog • **pages 13 and 14**

Use the **frog** writing form with books such as:

Commander Toad in Space by Jane Yolen; Demco Media, 1996.
Frog and Toad are Friends by Arnold Lobel; Harpercrest, 1987.
Frog Counts to Ten by John Leiber; Millbrook Press, 1995.
Froggie Went A-Courting by Chris Conover; Farrar, Straus & Giroux, 1988.
Hop Jump by Ellen Stoll Walsh; Harcourt Brace, 1995.

Cat • **pages 15 and 16**

Use the **cat** writing form with books such as:

Cookie's Week by Cindy Ward; Paper Star, 1997.
Cross Country Cat by Mary Calhoun; William Morrow and Company, 1979.
Mother Cat Has Three Kittens by Denise Fleming; Henry Holt and Company,
 1995.
My New Kitten by Joanna Cole; William Morrow and Company, 1995.
Only the Cat Saw by Ashley Wolff; Walker and Company, 1996.

Rabbit • **pages 17 and 18**

Use the **rabbit** writing form with books such as:

A Bedtime Story by Mem Fox; Mondo Publications, 1996.
The Bionic Bunny Show by Marc Brown; Little, Brown and Company, 1985.
Bunnicula by Deborah Howe; Demco Media, 1996.
Humbug Rabbit by Lorna Balian; Humbug Books, 1987.
The Tale of Peter Rabbit by Beatrix Potter; Warne, 1902.

Princess

Use the **princess** writing form with books such as:

Amazing Grace by Mary Hoffman; Dial Books for Young Readers, 1991.
Flossie and the Fox by Patricia C. McKissack; E. P. Dutton, 1986.
Frog Princess by Laura Cecil; Greenwillow, 1995.
The Paper Bag Princess by Michael Marchenko; Annick Press, 1995.
Princess Smartypants by Babette Cole; Putnam Publishing Group, 1987.

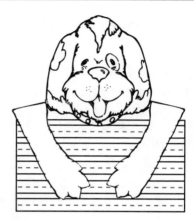

Dog

Use the **dog** writing form with books such as:

The Adventures of Taxi Dog by Debra Barracca and Sal Barracca; Dial Books for Young Readers, 1990.
Aldo Peanut Butter by Johanna Hurwitz; Puffin, 1992.
Angus and the Cat by Margorie Flack; Farrar, Straus & Giroux, 1997.
The First Dog by Jan Brett; Harcourt Brace, 1992.
Harry the Dirty Dog by Gene Zion; Harpercrest, 1987.

Bear

Use the **bear** writing form with books such as:

The Bear by Raymond Briggs; Random Library, 1994.
Big Bad Bruce by Bill Peet; Houghton Mifflin, 1982.
Brown Bear, Brown Bear, What Do You See? by Bill Martin; Henry Holt and Company, 1996.
Goldilocks and the Three Bears by Jan Brett; Paper Star, 1996.
I'm Terrific by Marjorie Weinman Sharmat; Holiday House, 1988.

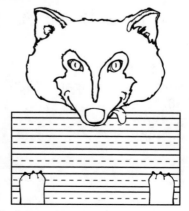

Wolf

Use the **wolf** writing form with books such as:

Can I Help? by Marilyn Janorvitz; North-South Books, 1998.
It's So Nice to Have a Wolf Around the House by Harry Allard; Picture Yearling, 1997.
Little Red Riding Hood: A Newfangled Prairie Tale by Lisa Campbell Ernst; Simon and Schuster, 1995.
Nicki and the Big, Bad Wolves by Valeri Gorbachev; Paper Star, 1998.
The Wolf's Chicken Stew by Keiko Lasza; Paper Star, 1996.

Old Lady •••••••••••••••••••••••••••••••• pages **27** and **28**

Use the **old lady** writing form with books such as:

Do Not Open by Brinton Turkle; E. P. Dutton, 1993.
I Know an Old Lady Who Swallowed a Pie by Alison Jackson; Dutton Books, 1997.
Nana Upstairs and Nana Downstairs by Tomie de Paola; Putnam Publishing Group, 1998.
Old Mother Hubbard and Her Wonderful Dog by James Marshall; Farrar, Straus & Giroux, 1991.
Wildred Gordon McDonald Partridge by Mem Fox; Kane/Miller, 1985.

Gingerbread Boy •••••••••••••••••••••• pages **29** and **30**

Use the **gingerbread boy** writing form with books such as:

The Gingerbread Boy by Paul Galdone; Clarion Books, 1983.
The Gingerbread Boy by Richard Egielski; HarperCollins, 1997.
The Gingerbread Rabbit by Randall Jarrell; HarperCollins, 1996.

Prince •••••••••••••••••••••••••••••••••••• pages **31** and **32**

Use the **prince** writing form with books such as:

The 500 Hats of Bartholomew Cubbins by Dr. Seuss; Random Library, 1990.
Alexander and the Terrible, Horrible, No Good, Very Bad Day by Judith Viorst; Aladdin Paperbacks, 1987.
A Boy Wants a Dinosaur by Hiawyn Oram; Sunburst, 1993.
Prince Cinders by Babette Cole; Putnam Publishing Group, 1997.
Prince Peter and the Teddy Bear by David McKee; Farrar, Straus & Giroux, 1997.

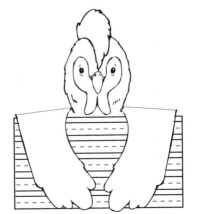

Chicken •••••••••••••••••••••••••••••••••• pages **33** and **34**

Use the **chicken** writing form with books such as:

Big Egg by Molly Coxe; Random House, 1997.
The Chicken Sisters by Laura Joffe Numeroff; HarperCollins, 1997.
Emma's Eggs by Margariet Ruurs; Stoddart Kids, 1997.
Hattie and the Fox by Mem Fox; Aladdin Paperbacks, 1992.
The Little Red Hen by Margot Zemach; Farrar, Straus & Giroux, 1983.
Rosie's Walk by Pat Hutchins; Little Simon, 1998.

Hippo

Use the **hippo** writing form with books such as:

Am I Beautiful? by Else Holmelund Minarik; Greenwillow, 1992.
The Blushful Hippopotamus by Chris Baschka; Orchard Books, 1996.
George and Martha: The Complete Stories of Two Best Friends by James
    Marshall; Houghton Mifflin Company, 1997.
The Happy Hippopotami by Bill Martin; Harcourt Brace, 1992.
I Had a Hippopotamus by Hector Viveros; Lee & Low Books, 1998.
Never Babysit the Hippopotamuses! by Doug Johnson; Owlet, 1997.

Mice

Use the **mice** writing form with books such as:

Angelina Ballerina by Katherine Holabird; Crown Publications, 1983.
A Beautiful Feast for a Big King Cat by John Archambault; Harper
    Trophy, 1996.
Frederick by Leo Lionni; Knopf, 1990.
If You Give a Mouse a Cookie by Laura Joffe Numberoff;
    HarperCollins, 1985.
Mousekin's Lost Woodland by Edna Miller; Silver Burdett and Ginn, 1996.

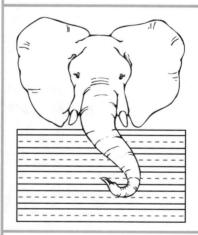

Elephant

Use the **elephant** writing form with books such as:

Babar and His Children by Jean De Brunhoff; Random House, 1988.
Baby Elephant by Lucille Recht Penner; Grosset and Dunlap, 1997.
Bashi, Elephant Baby by Theresa Radcliffe; Viking Childrens Books, 1998.
The Elephant's Child by Lorinda Bryan Cauley; Harcourt Brace
    Jovanovich, 1988.
Horton Hatches a Who! by Dr. Seuss; Random House, 1954.

Giant

Use the **giant** writing form with books such as:

Book of Giants and Little People by Diane Goode; Dutton Books, 1997.
Boy Soup: Or When Giant Caught Cold by Loris Lesynski; Annick
    Press, 1996.
The Giant by Nicholas Heller; Greenwillow, 1997.
The Great Quillow by James Thurber; Harcourt Brace, 1994.
Jack and the Beanstalk by Steven Kellogg; Mulberry Books, 1997.

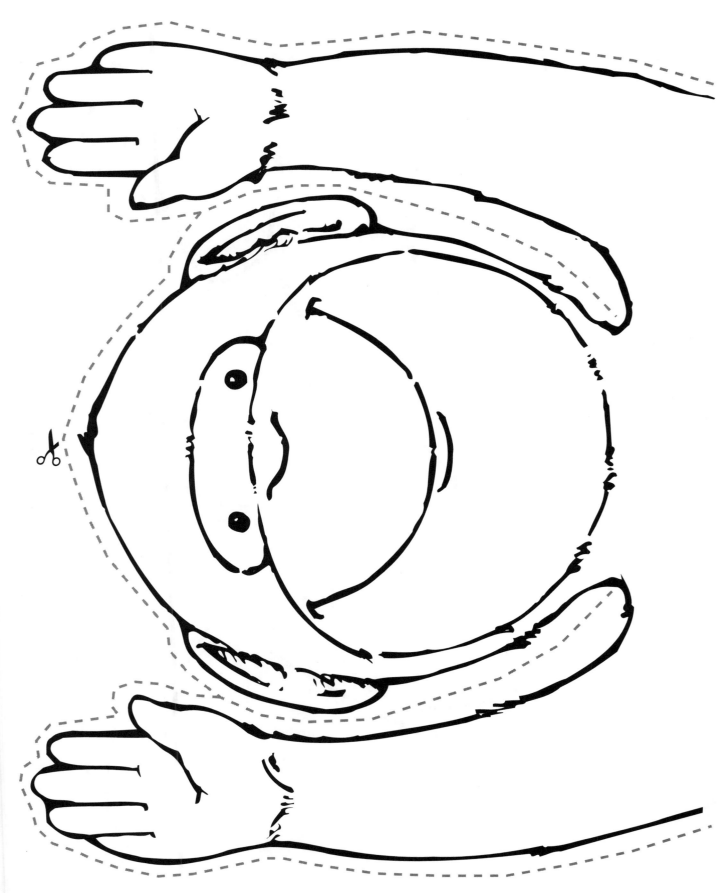

7

Paste along this edge.

Monkey

Writing Forms • EMC 596

9

Paste along this edge.

Paste along this edge.

Pig

Writing Forms • EMC 596

©1999 by Evan-Moor Corp.

10

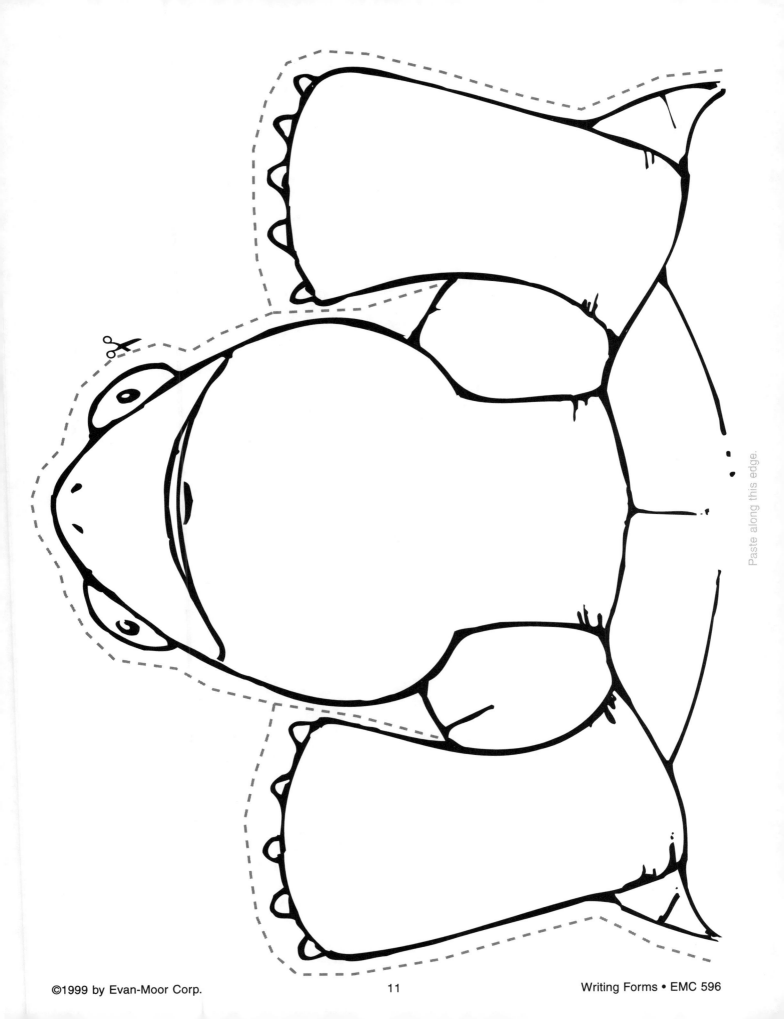

11

Writing Forms • EMC 596

Paste along this edge.

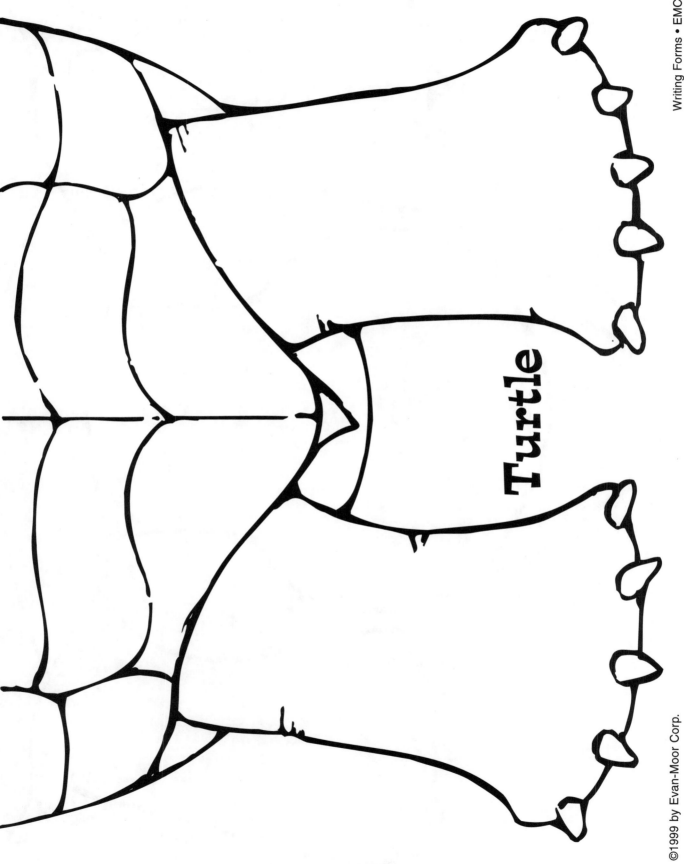

Turtle

Writing Forms • EMC 596

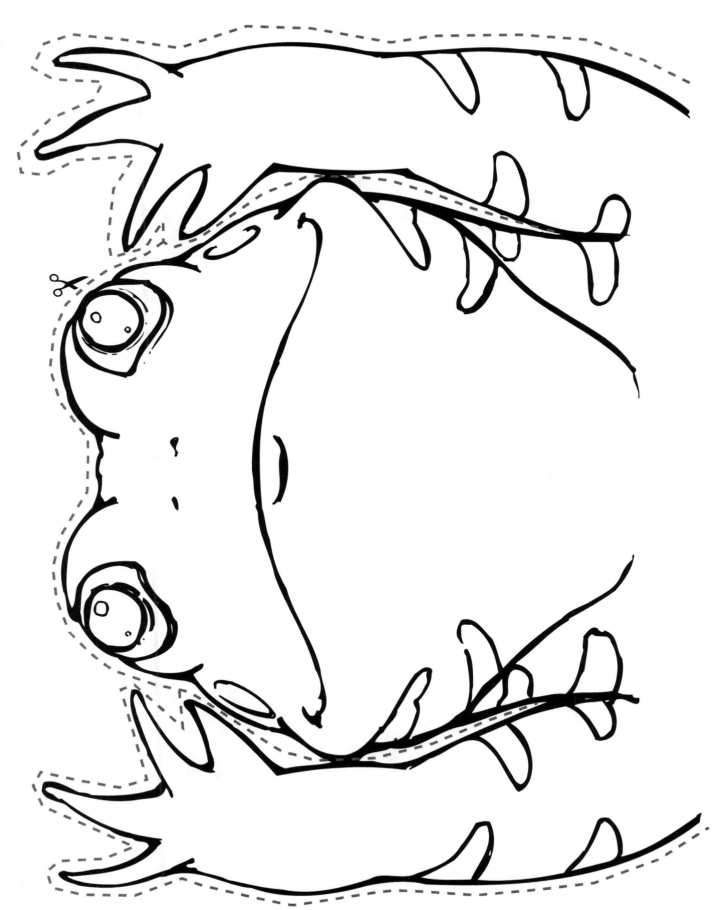

13

Writing Forms • EMC 596

Paste along this edge.

Frog

Writing Forms • EMC 596

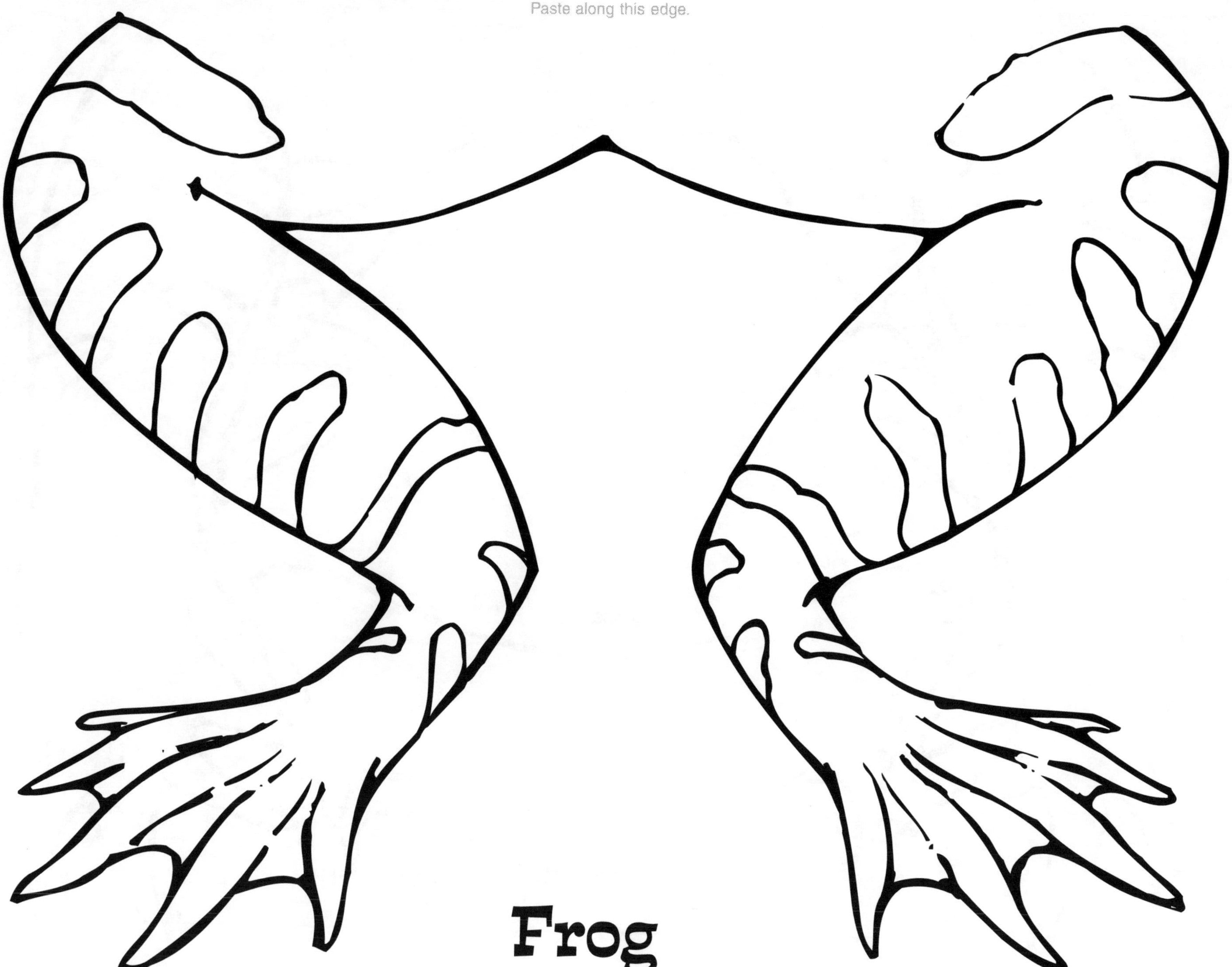

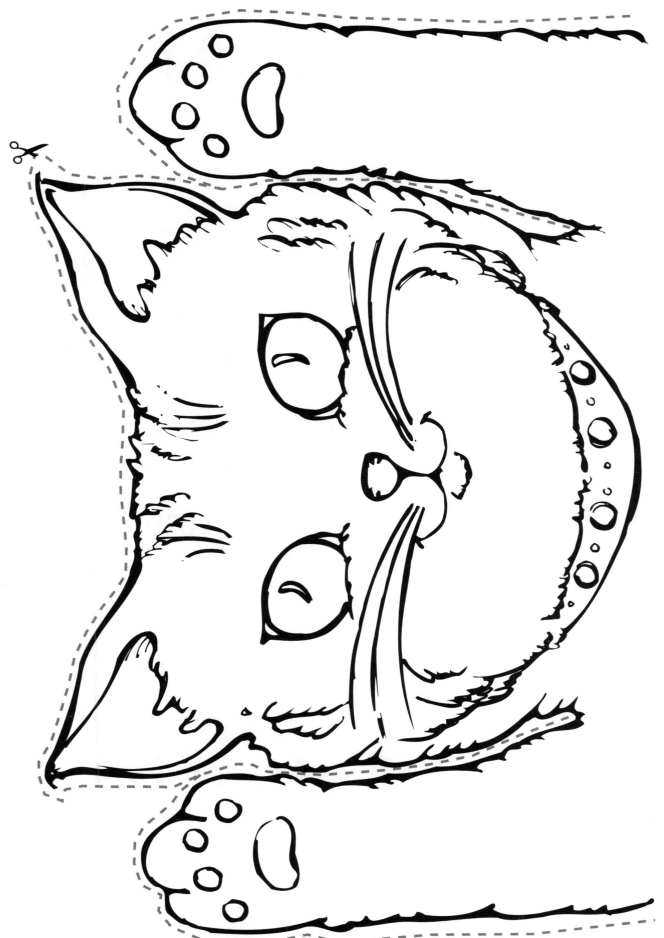

Paste along this edge.

Writing Forms • EMC 596

Cat

Writing Forms • EMC 596

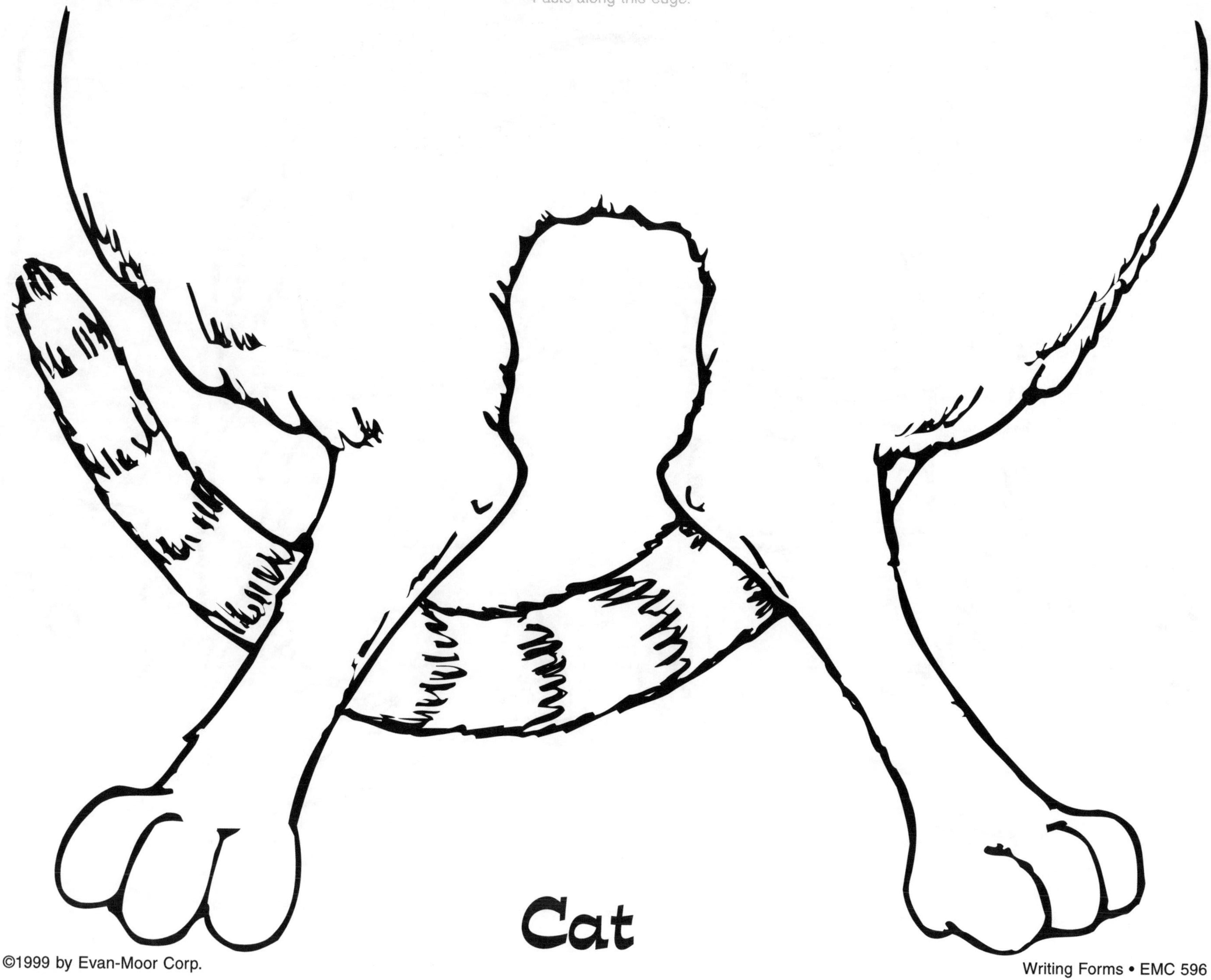

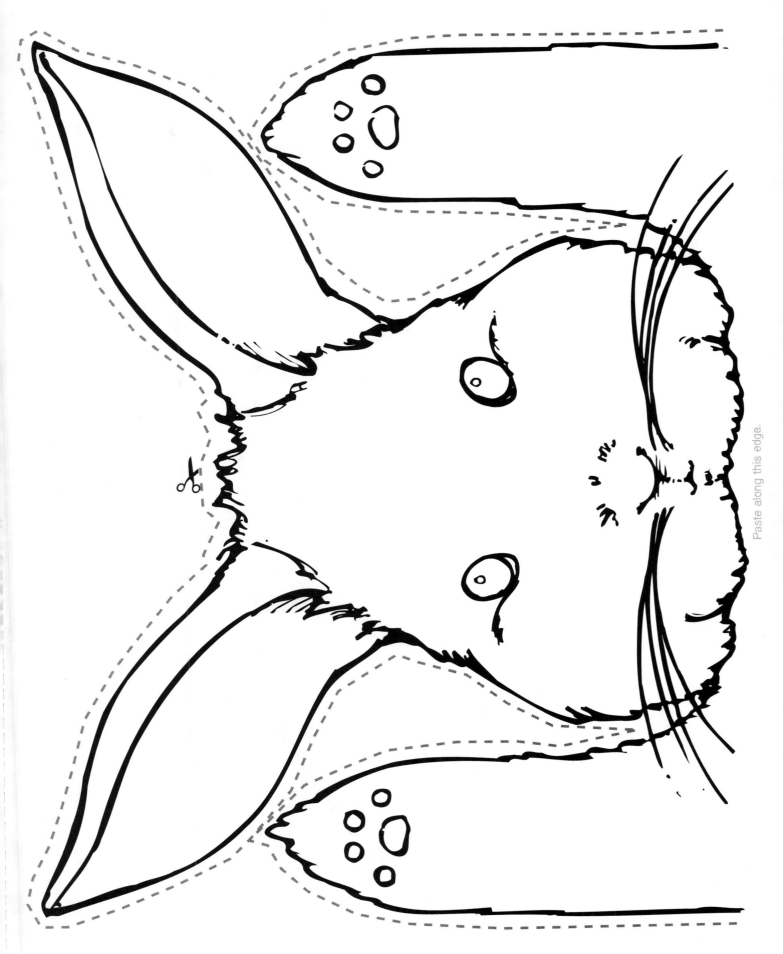

Writing Forms • EMC 596

Paste along this edge.

Writing Forms • EMC 596

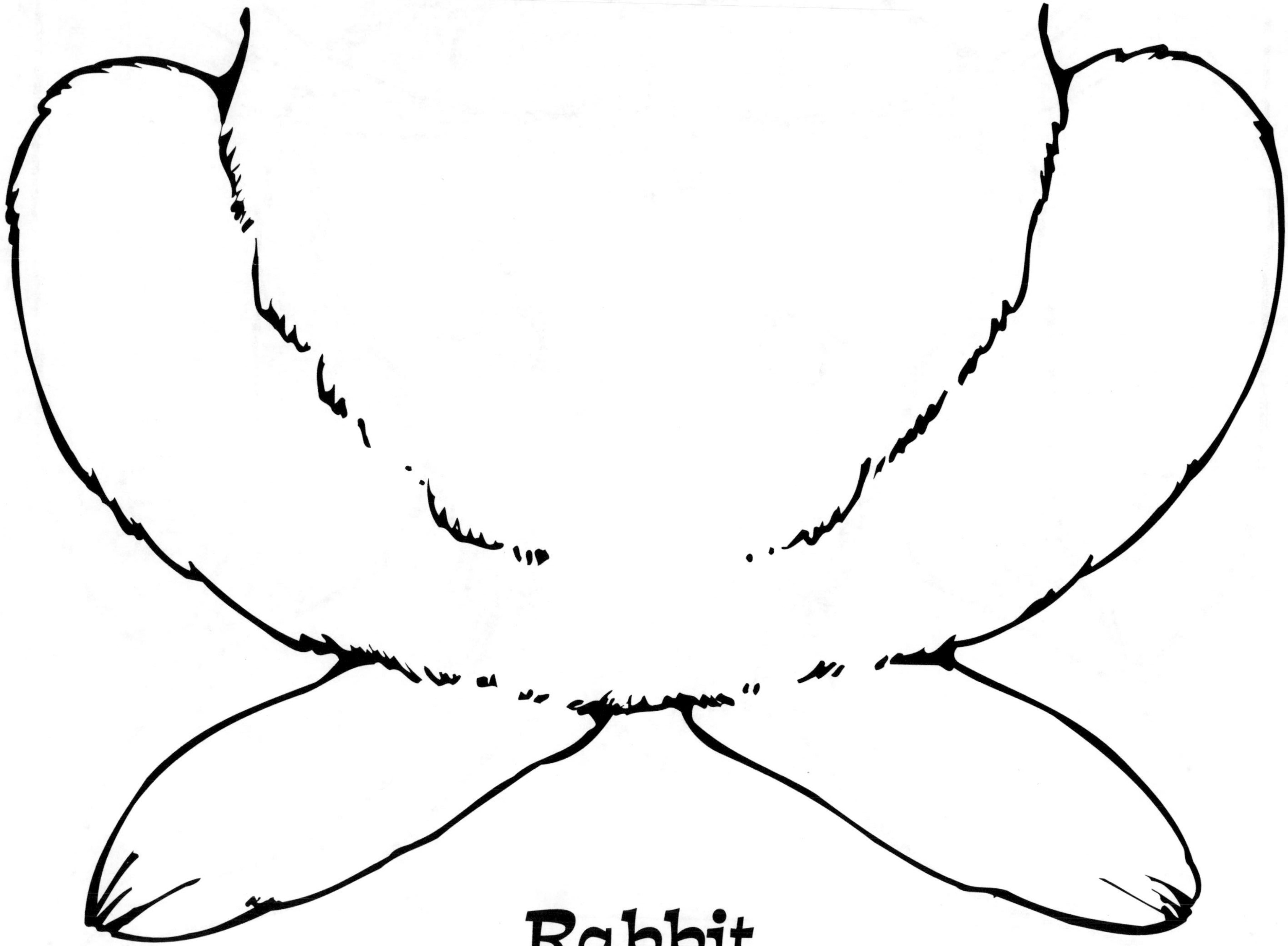

Rabbit

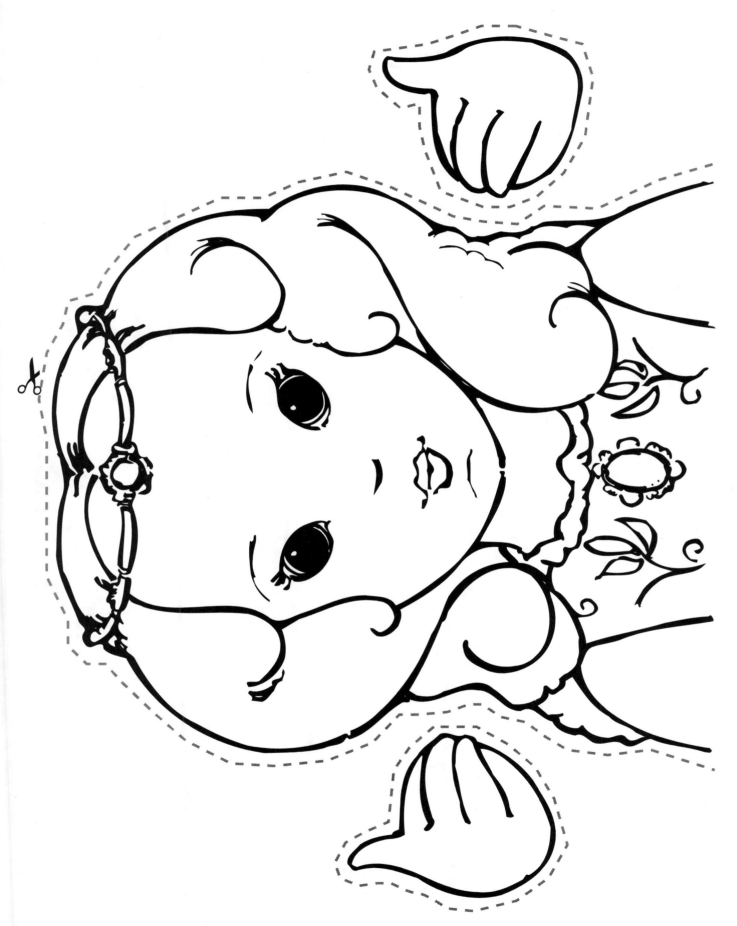

Paste along this edge.

Writing Forms • EMC 596

Princess

Writing Forms • EMC 596

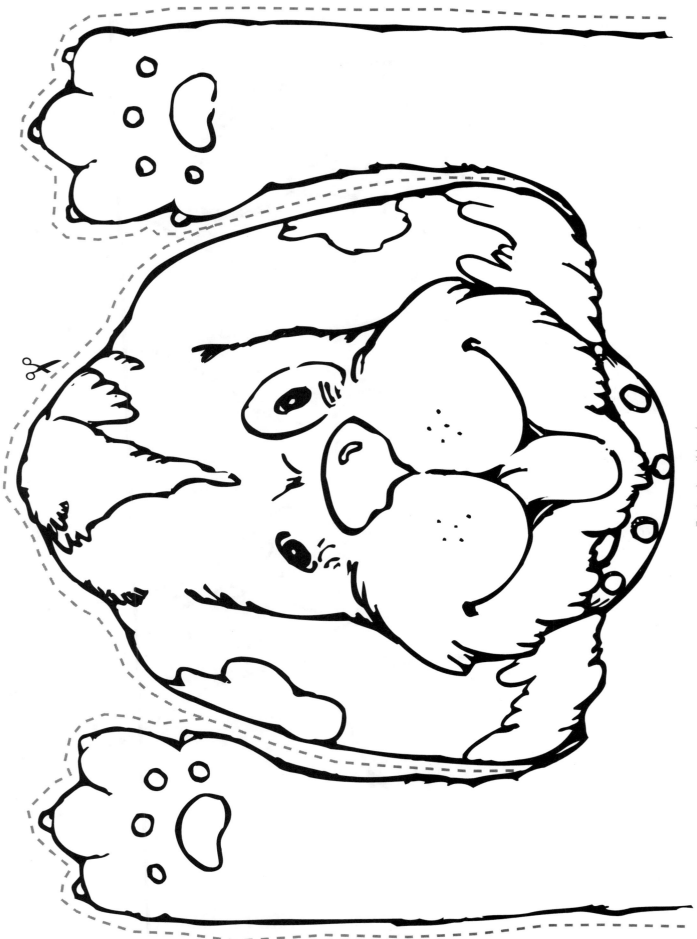

Paste along this edge.

Writing Forms • EMC 596

Dog

Writing Forms • EMC 596

22

Paste along this edge.

Bear

24

Paste along this edge.

Writing Forms • EMC 596

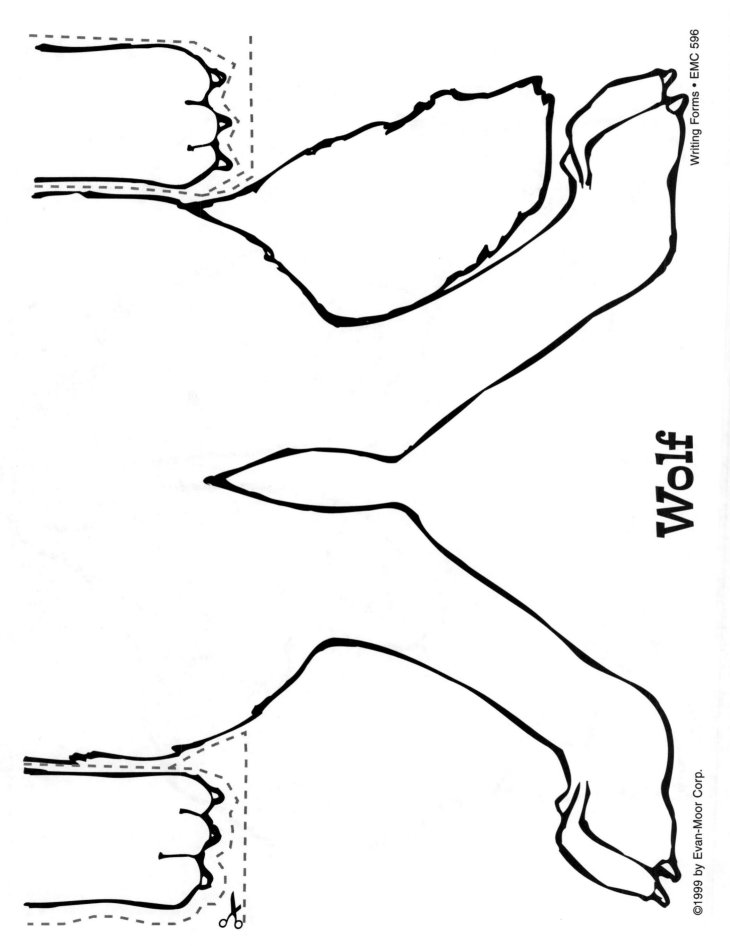

Wolf

Paste along this edge.

Writing Forms • EMC 596

©1999 by Evan-Moor Corp.

26

Paste along this edge.

Writing Forms • EMC 596

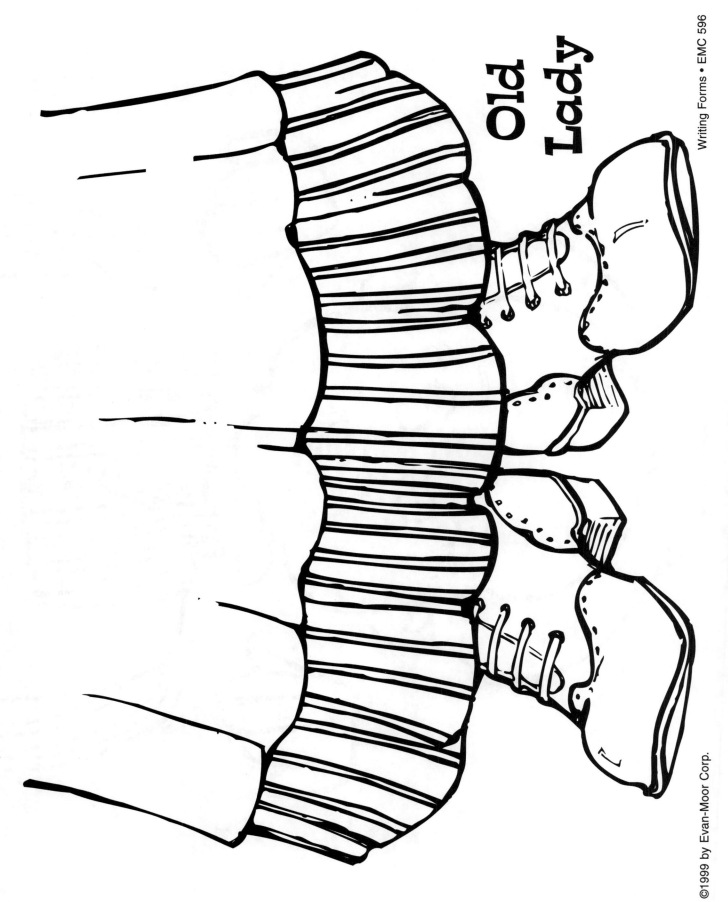

Old Lady

Writing Forms • EMC 596

28

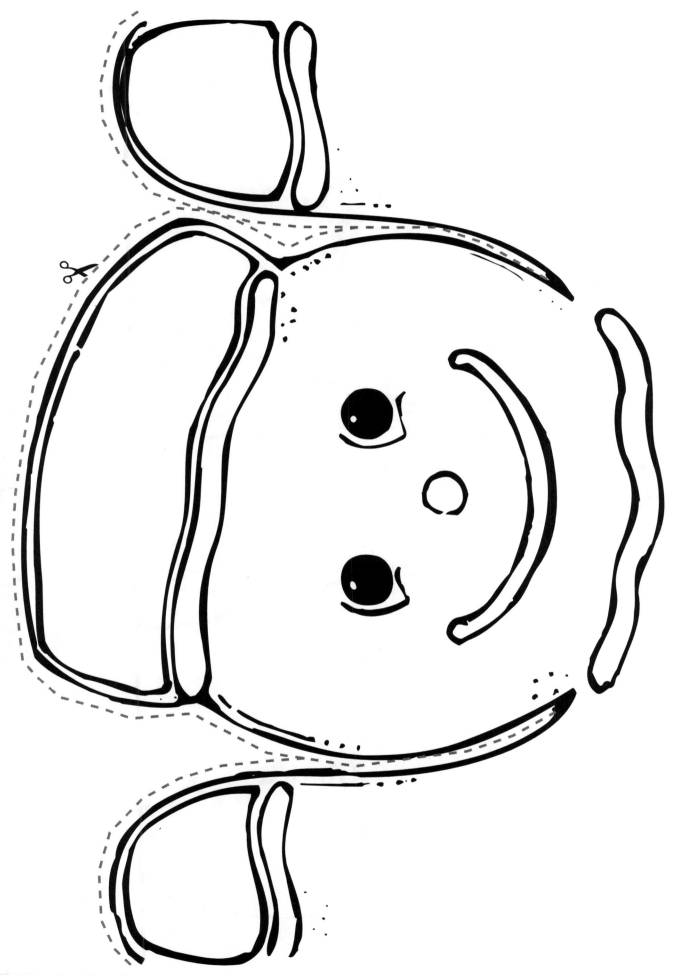

Paste along this edge.

Writing Forms • EMC 596

Paste along this edge.

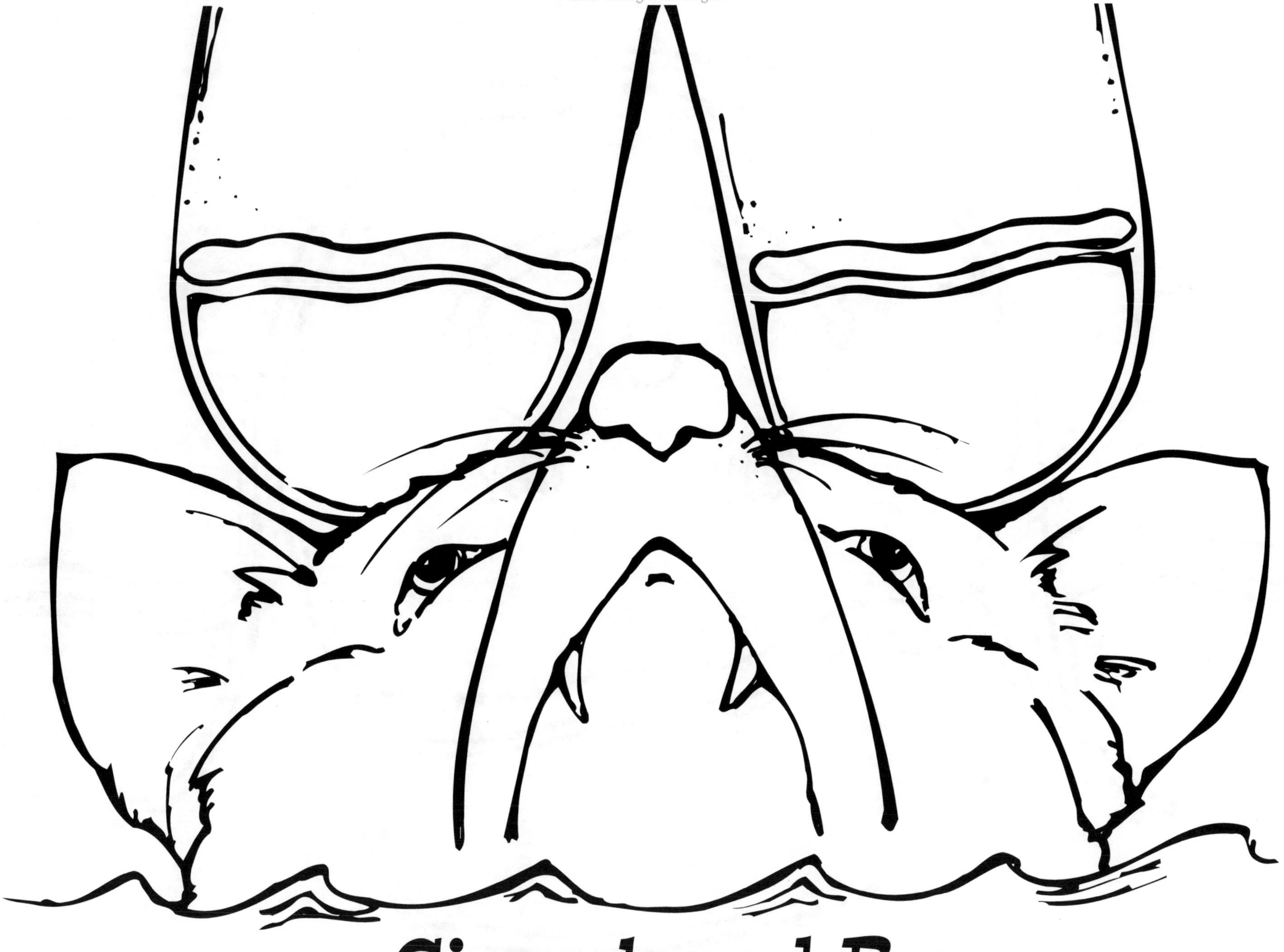

Gingerbread Boy

Writing Forms • EMC 596

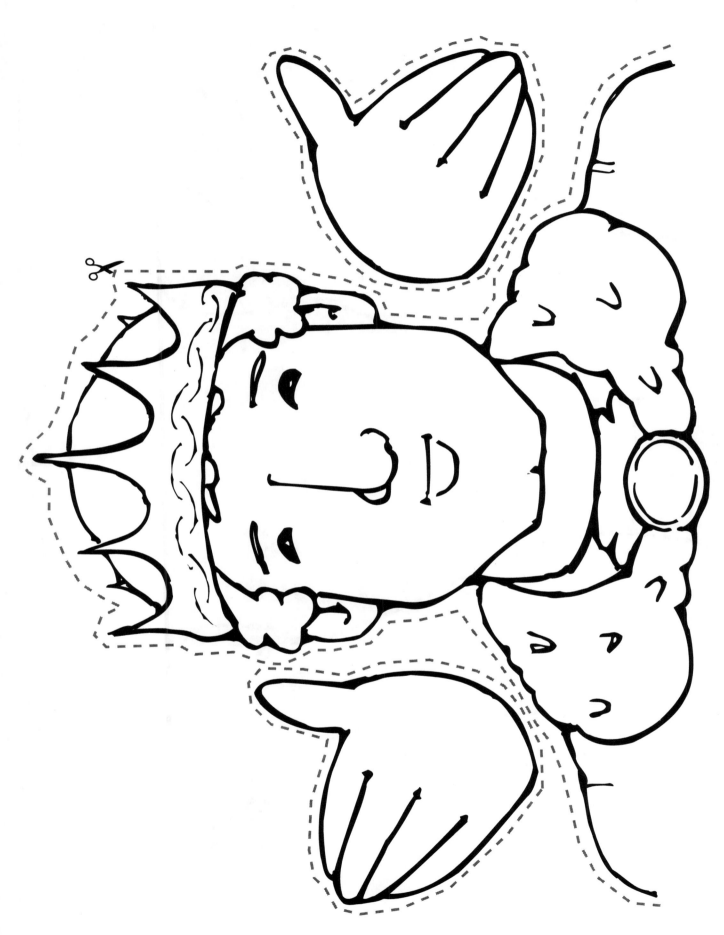

31

Writing Forms • EMC 596

Paste along this edge.

Prince

Writing Forms • EMC 596

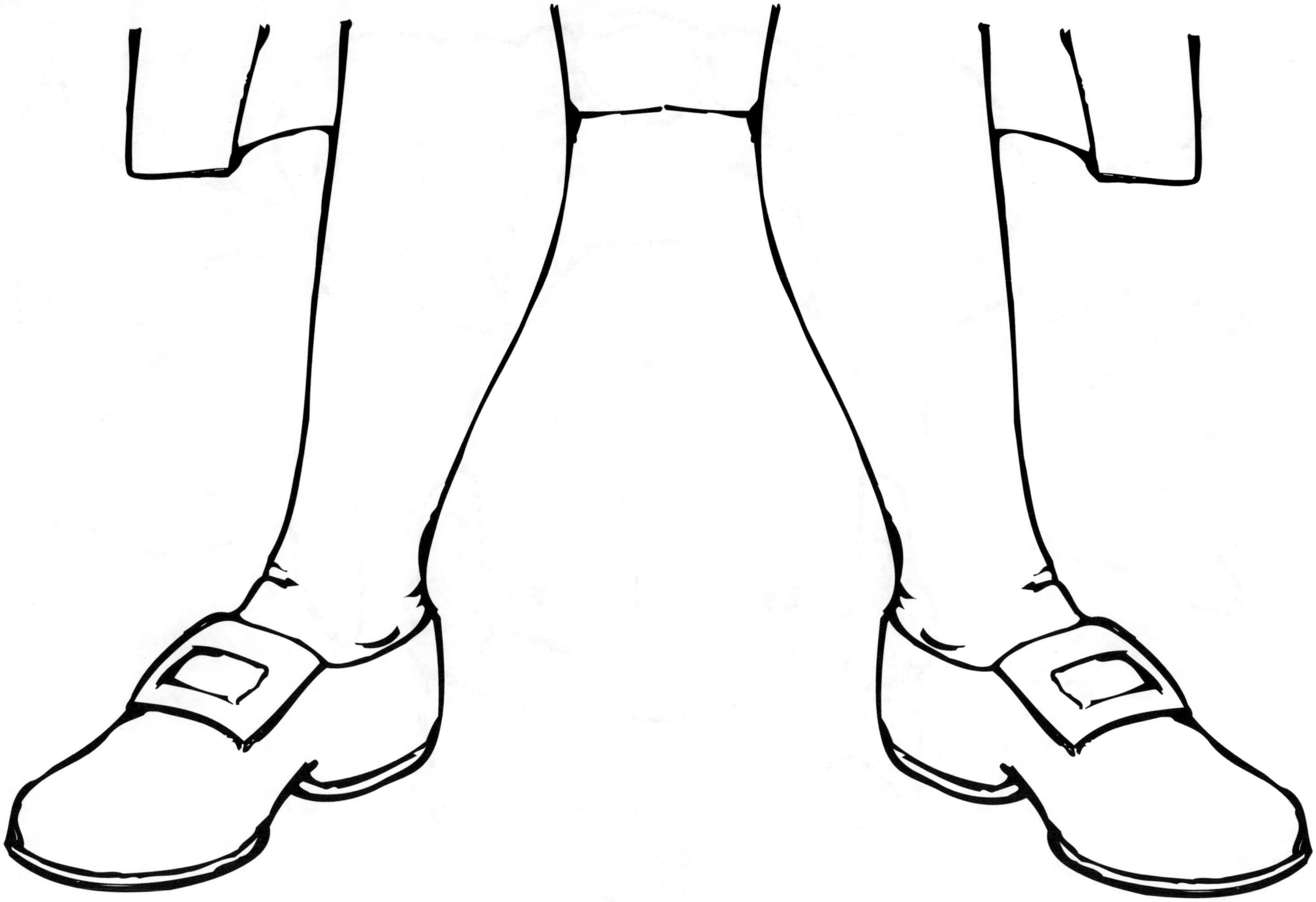

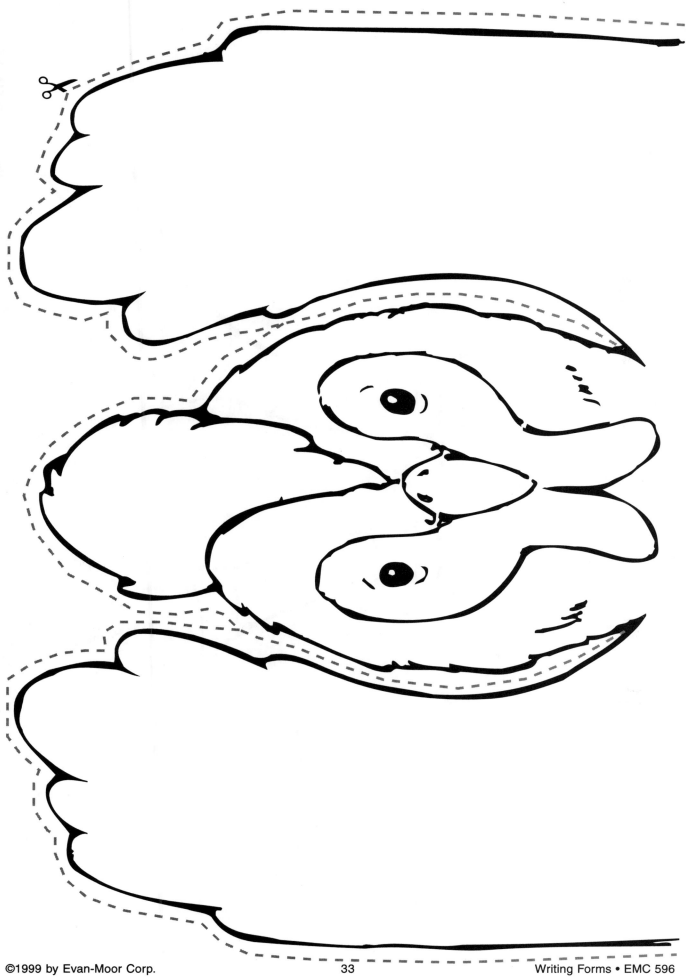

Paste along this edge.

Writing Forms • EMC 596

Chicken

Paste along this edge.

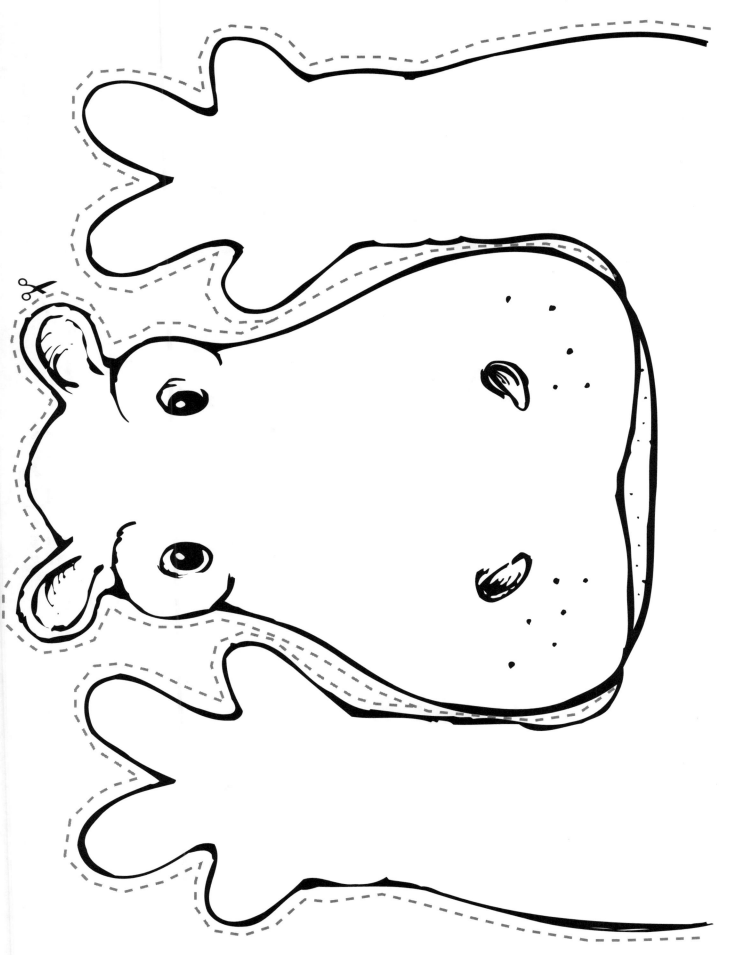

Paste along this edge.

35

Writing Forms • EMC 596

Hippo

Writing Forms • EMC 596

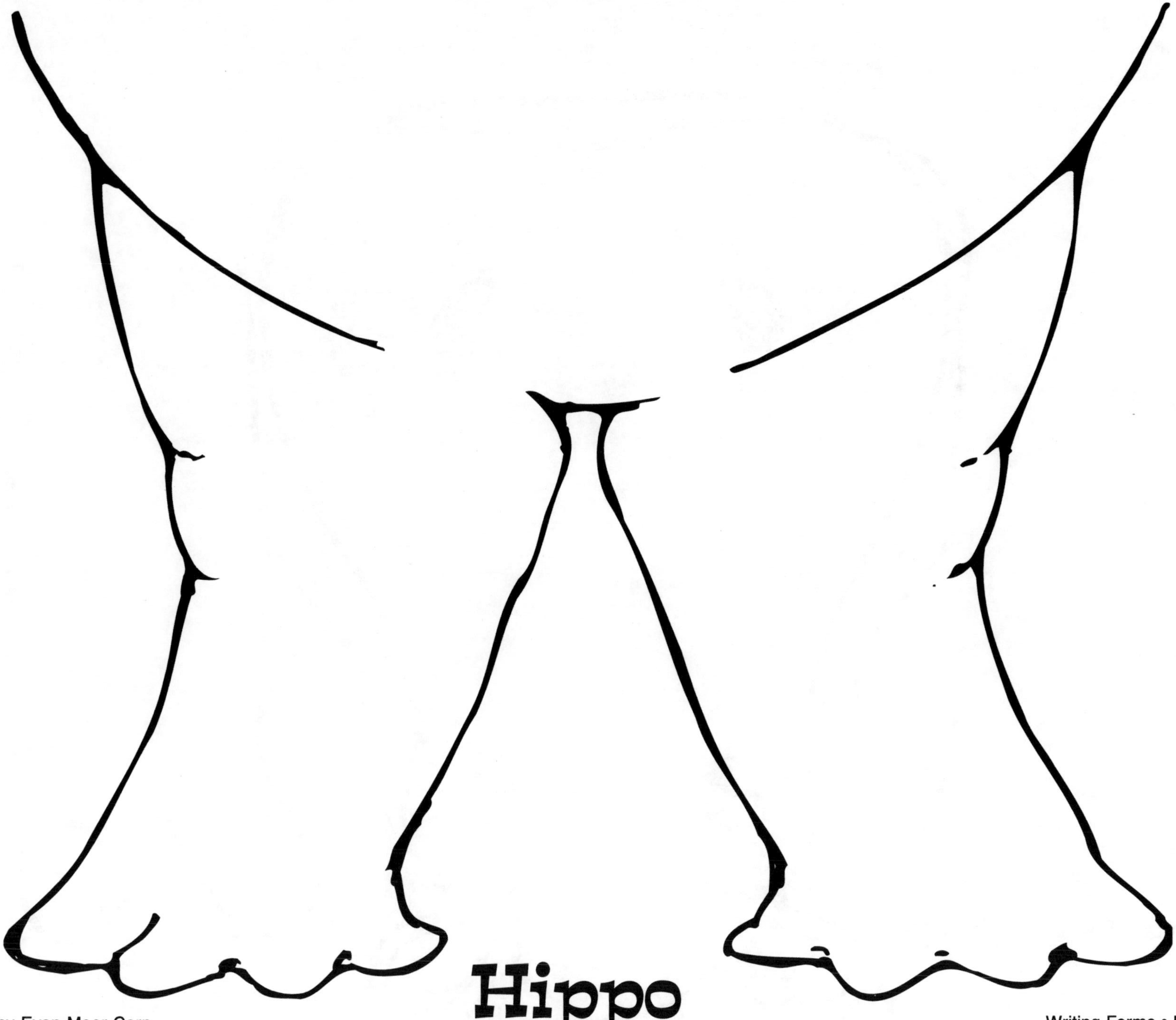

Paste along this edge.

Writing Forms • EMC 596

Mice

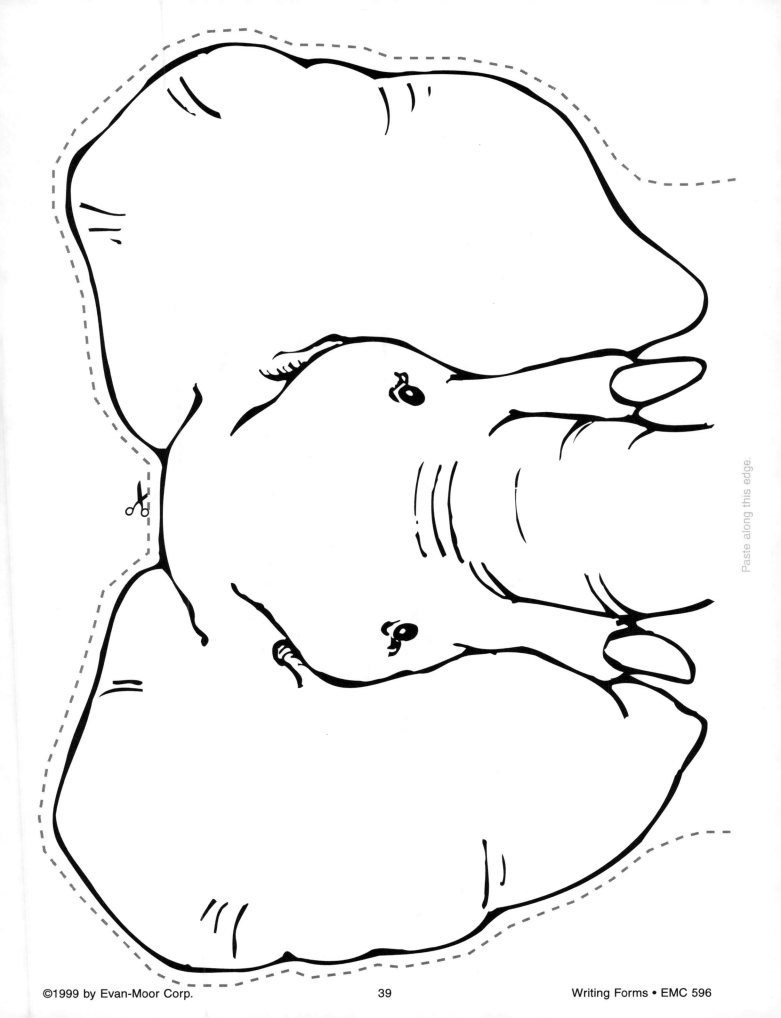

Writing Forms • EMC 596

Paste along this edge.

Paste along this edge.

Elephant

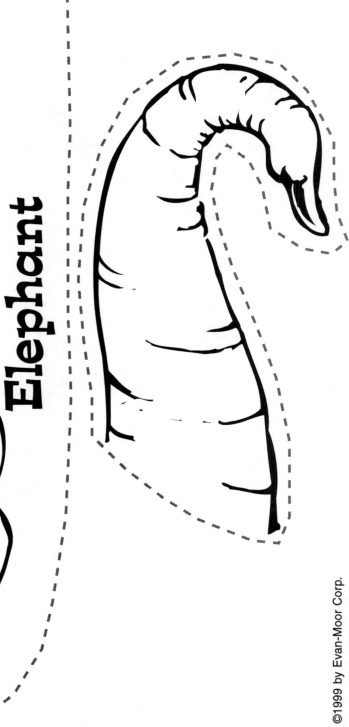

Writing Forms • EMC 596

©1999 by Evan-Moor Corp.

40

Trace around your hand. Cut it out and paste it here.

Trace around your hand. Cut it out and paste it here.

Paste along this edge.

Writing Forms • EMC 596

Giant

Writing Forms • EMC 596

Holiday Writing Forms

Holiday writing forms can be used to:

- write original stories
- copy a seasonal poem
- list facts about the holiday
- practice handwriting
- hold student work on a bulletin board display
- decorate a bulletin board
- create a cover for a class book

Cut out the "top."

Paste your own paper to the "top."

Paste the "bottom" to your paper.

A Bear for All Seasons •••••••••••••••• pages 49 and 50

(Draw an appropriate symbol for the season [heart, egg, etc.] and paste it to the bear's hand.)

Story starters:

It is almost Easter and the Easter Bunny is sick. How can Bear help?

Bear went to Ireland for a vacation. "I think I'll try to catch a leprechaun," Bear decided.

Help Bear write a letter to Santa Claus.

"I want to make special valentines for all my animal friends," said Bear.

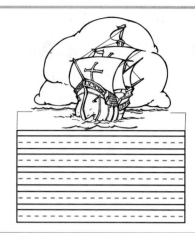

Christopher Columbus .... pages 51 and 52

Story starters:

Why did Columbus set sail across the Atlantic Ocean?
Why was Columbus's crew nervous about the voyage?
What did Columbus discover when he reached land?
What would it be like to sail on the Santa Maria?

Ghost .... pages 53 and 54

Story starters:

Last night was the spookiest Halloween ever.
Toby was a shy little ghost and this was his first Halloween night.
Let me tell you how to trick a ghost.
This is how to make a ghost costume.

Turkey .... pages 55 and 56

Story starters:

How do you catch a wild turkey?
Describe the smells of Thanksgiving.
"You won't be Thanksgiving dinner," John promised his pet turkey.
This is what happened at the first Thanksgiving dinner.

Pilgrim Girl .... pages 57 and 58

Story starters:

If I were a Pilgrim girl....
How did the Pilgrim children help to settle the new land?
Pretend you were a girl on the Mayflower. Write about the journey.
What do you think a Pilgrim girl would be thankful for?

Pilgrim Boy ••••••••••••••••••••••••••••• pages 59 and 60

Story starters:

If I were a Pilgrim boy....
What do you think happened when the first Native American
   child and the first Pilgrim child met?
Describe how it would feel to be a boy in a wild, new land.
Father and I went out early to capture a wild turkey

Native American Boy ••••••••••••••••••••••••• pages 61 and 62

Story starters:

How would a Native American boy explain popcorn to the Pilgrim children?
What kinds of games did Native American children play?
What do you think you would be doing if you were a
   Native American boy in 1620?

Native American Girl ••••••••••••••••••••••••• pages 63 and 64

Story starters

What do you think you would be doing if you were a
   Native American girl in 1620?
How did a Native American girl help her family?
What did the Pilgrims learn from the Native Americans?

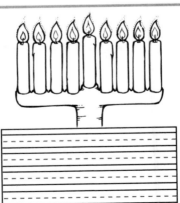

Menorah ••••••••••••••••••••••••••••••••••••• pages 65 and 66

Story starters:

Describe a menorah and tell how it is used.
What happens at a Hanukkah celebration?
This is how you play with a dreidel.
The best part of Hanukkah is....

Santa ▪▪▪▪▪▪▪▪▪▪▪▪▪▪▪▪▪▪▪▪▪▪▪▪▪▪▪▪▪ **pages 67 and 68**

Story starters:

Describe how Santa Claus feels on Christmas morning after
    traveling around the world delivering gifts.
"This is how I help Santa Claus," said the little elf.
This is my Christmas wish for Santa Claus.
"All I want for Christmas is…."

Angel ▪▪▪▪▪▪▪▪▪▪▪▪▪▪▪▪▪▪▪▪▪▪▪▪▪▪▪▪▪ **pages 69 and 70**

Story starters:

Tell how the Littlest Angel won her wings.
What does an angel look like?
"This is what happened at the first Christmas," explained the angel.

Dr. Martin Luther King, Jr. ▪▪▪▪▪▪▪▪▪▪▪▪ **pages 71 and 72**

Story starters:

Why is Dr. Martin Luther King, Jr. remembered?
What was Dr. King's dream for his people?
What wish do you have for the people of the world?

Groundhog ▪▪▪▪▪▪▪▪▪▪▪▪▪▪▪▪▪▪▪▪▪▪▪ **pages 73 and 74**

Story starters:

What happens when the groundhog sees its shadow on February 2nd?
Describe a shadow.
Write a story about a brave groundhog.
The groundhog was afraid of its shadow. What are you afraid of?

Abraham Lincoln .... pages 75 and 76

Story starters:

Who was Abraham Lincoln?
If I could talk to Abraham Lincoln, I would ask....
Why was Abraham Lincoln called Honest Abe?
When Abraham Lincoln was a boy....

Cupid .... pages 77 and 78

Story starters:

How do you make a valentine?
Describe the best valentine you ever received.
What do we celebrate on Valentine's Day?
What is Cupid's job?

George Washington .... pages 79 and 80

Story starters:

This is what I know about George Washington.
Why was George Washington called the "Father of his country"?
If I could talk to George Washington, I would ask....

Leprechaun .... pages 81 and 82

Story starters:

"Where shall we look for the leprechaun's treasure?" asked Shawn.
Describe a leprechaun and its magical powers.
How would you catch a leprechaun?
This is how to make a leprechaun's favorite soup.

Easter Bunny ▪▪▪▪▪▪▪▪▪▪▪▪▪▪▪▪▪▪▪▪▪▪ pages 83 and 84

Story starters:

Write directions to your house for the Easter Bunny.
This is how to dye an Easter egg.
"Look what I found in my Easter basket," said (child's name).
Write about what your family does to celebrate Easter.

Happy Birthday Cake ▪▪▪▪▪▪▪▪▪▪▪▪▪▪▪ pages 85 and 86

Story starters:

Describe the best birthday party you ever had.
Plan a birthday party for the little puppy.
   Who will come?
   What will you eat?
   What games will you play?
"This is the worst birthday I ever had!"

Note: Draw an appropriate symbol for the season (heart, egg, etc.) and paste it to the bear's paw.

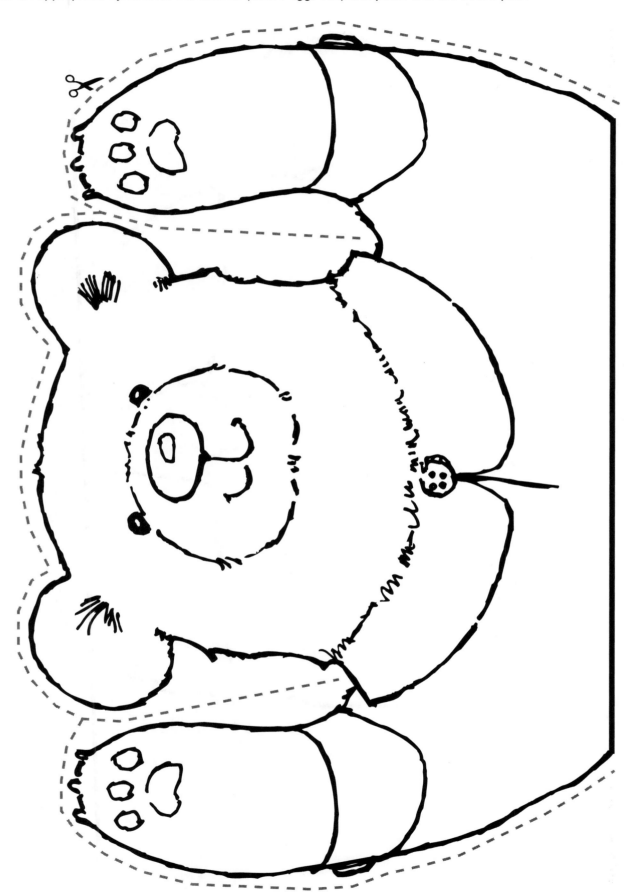

Paste along this edge

49

Paste along this edge.

A Bear for All Seasons

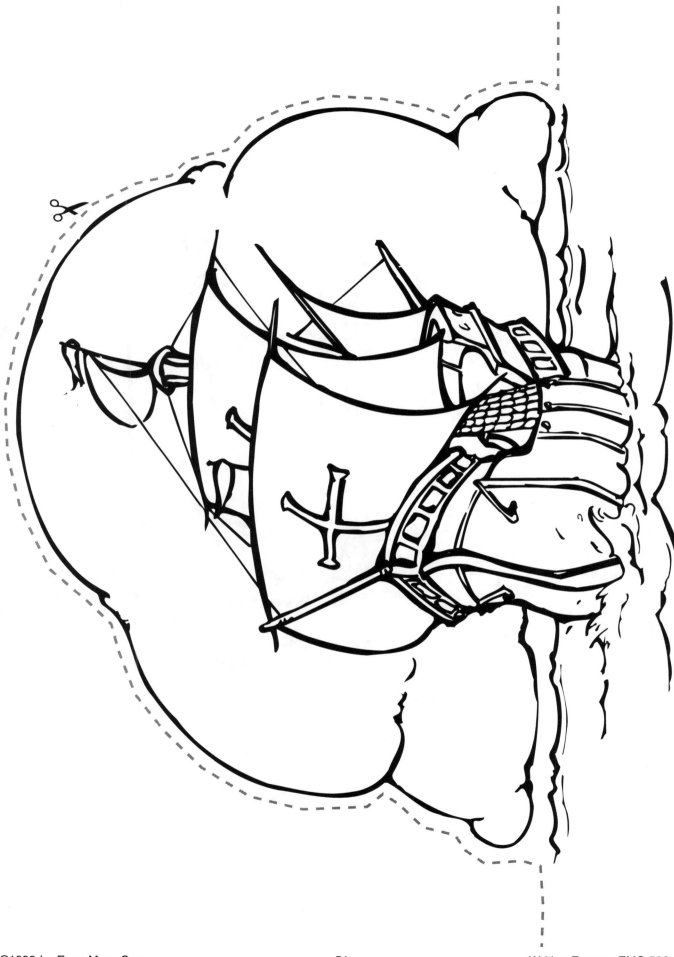

Paste along this edge.

Writing Forms • EMC 596

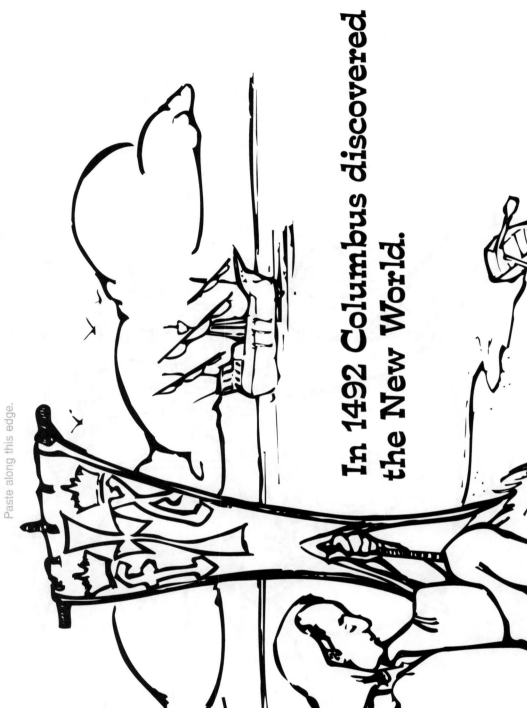

In 1492 Columbus discovered the New World.

Christopher Columbus

Writing Forms • EMC 596

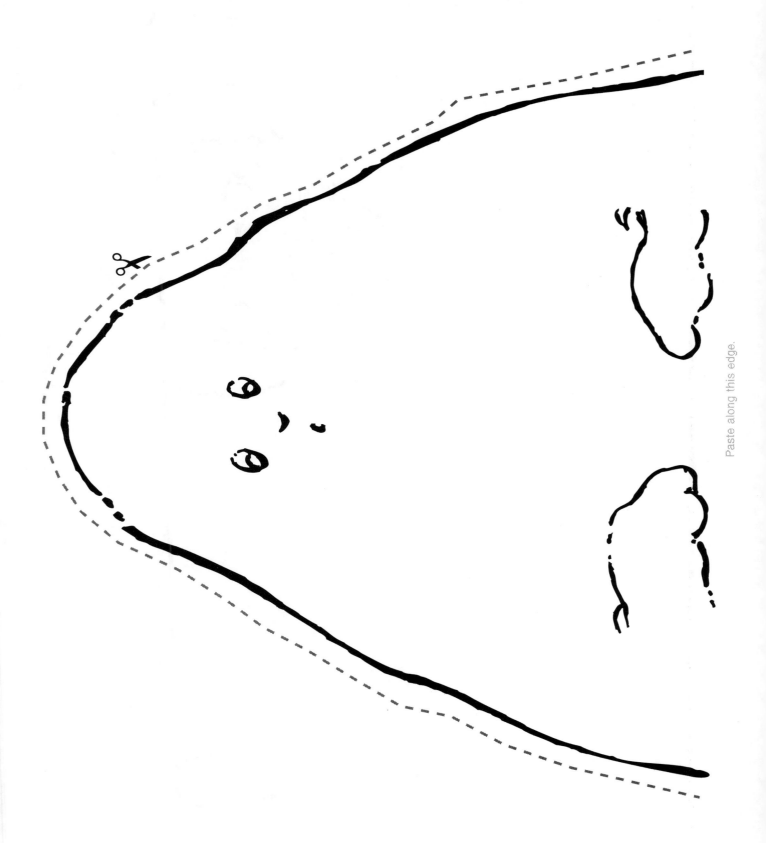

Paste along this edge.

53

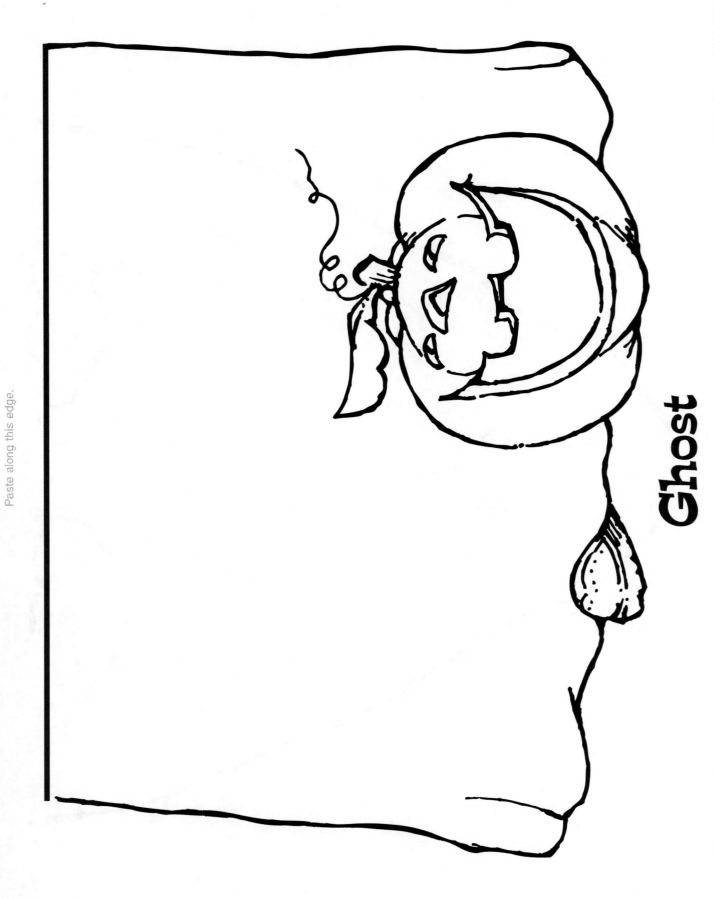

Ghost

Writing Forms • EMC 596

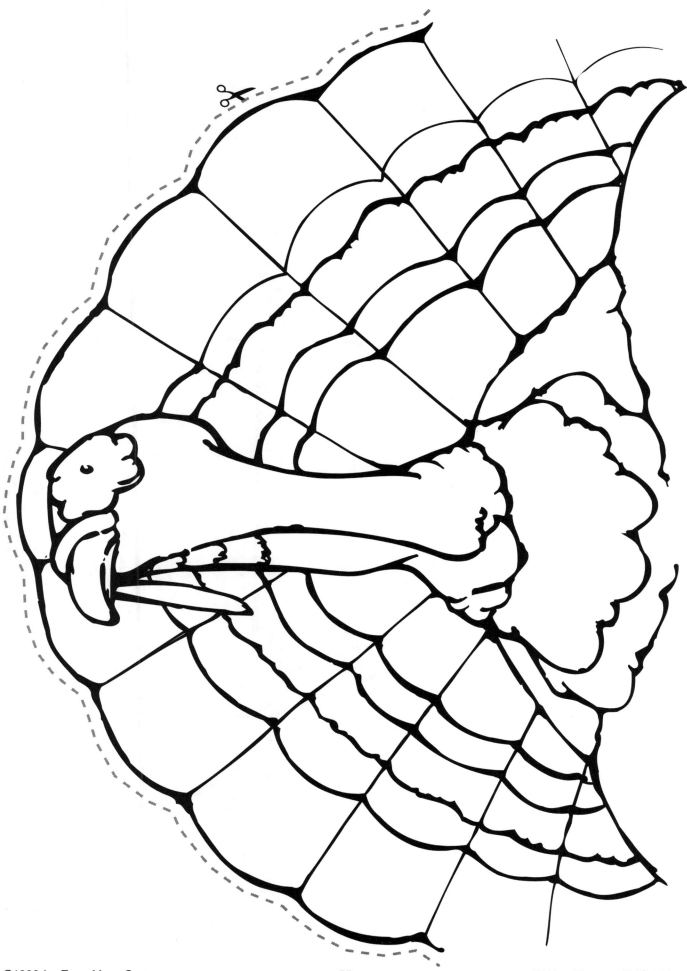

Paste along this edge.

Writing Forms • EMC 596

Turkey

Writing Forms • EMC 596

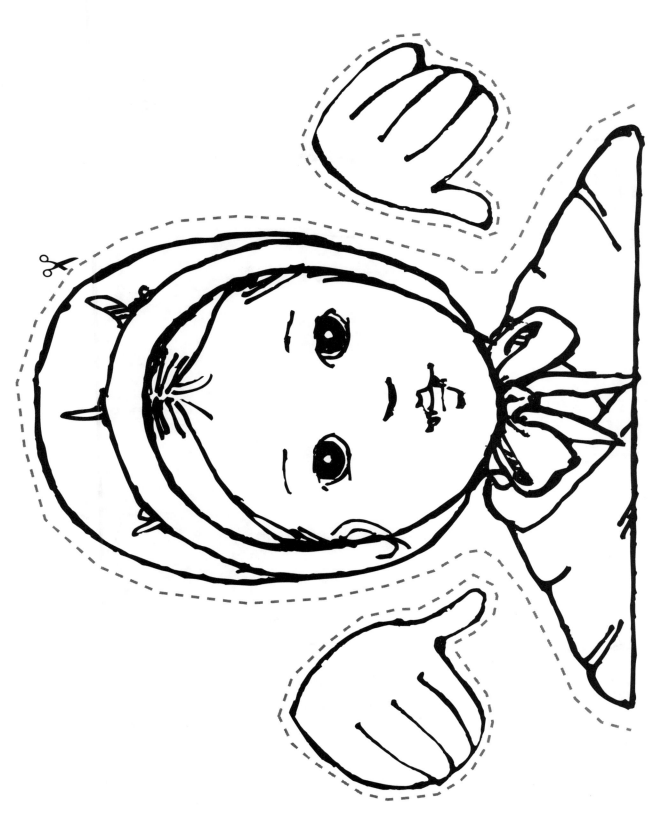

Paste along this edge.

Writing Forms • EMC 596

Paste along this edge.

Pilgrim Girl

Paste along this edge.

59

Pilgrim Boy

Paste along this edge.

61

Paste along this edge.

Native American Boy

Paste along this edge.

63

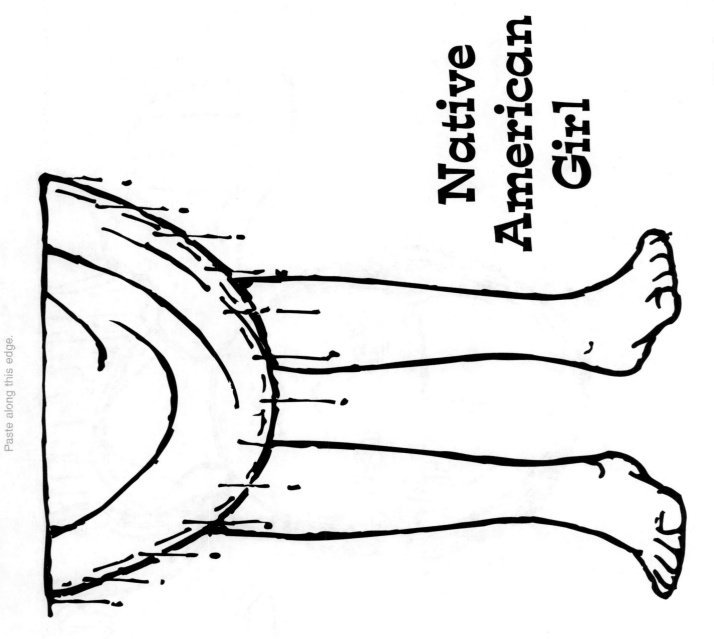

Native American Girl

Writing Forms • EMC 596

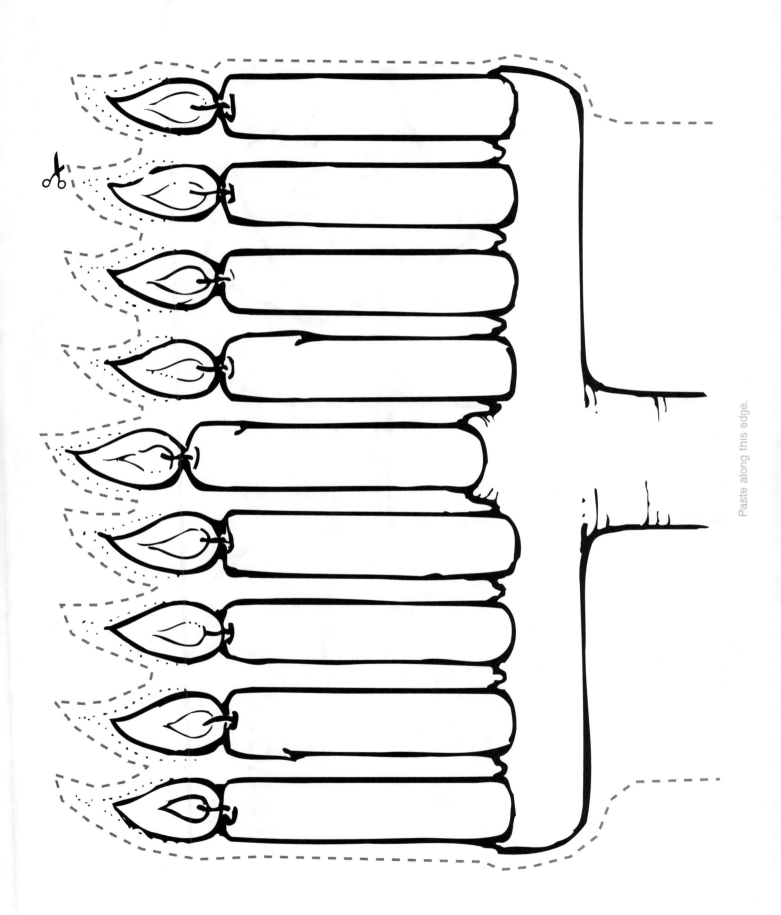

Paste along this edge.

Writing Forms • EMC 596

Paste along this edge.

Menorah

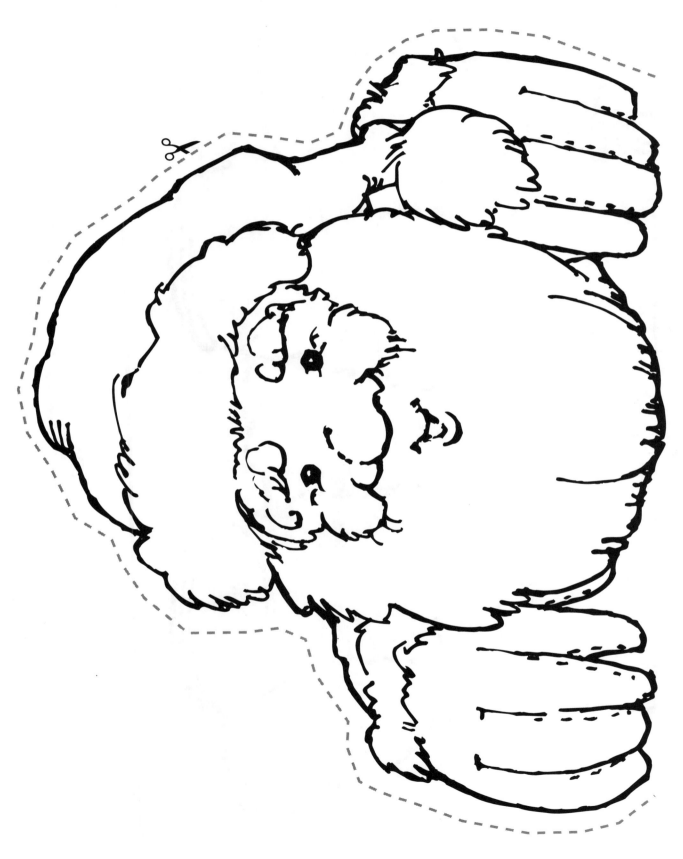

Paste along this edge.

Writing Forms • EMC 596

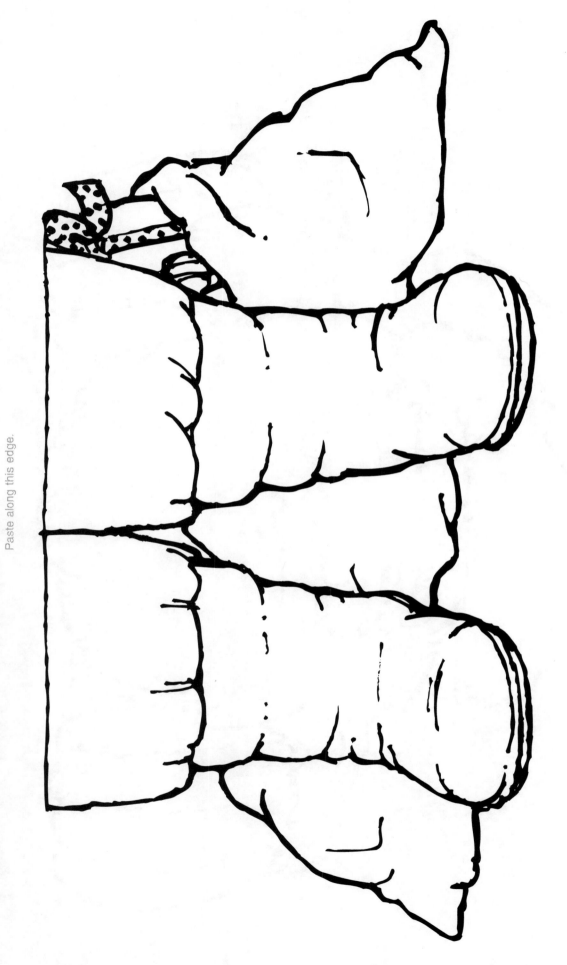

Paste along this edge.

Santa

Writing Forms • EMC 596

Paste along this edge.

Writing Forms • EMC 596

Writing Forms • EMC 596

Angel

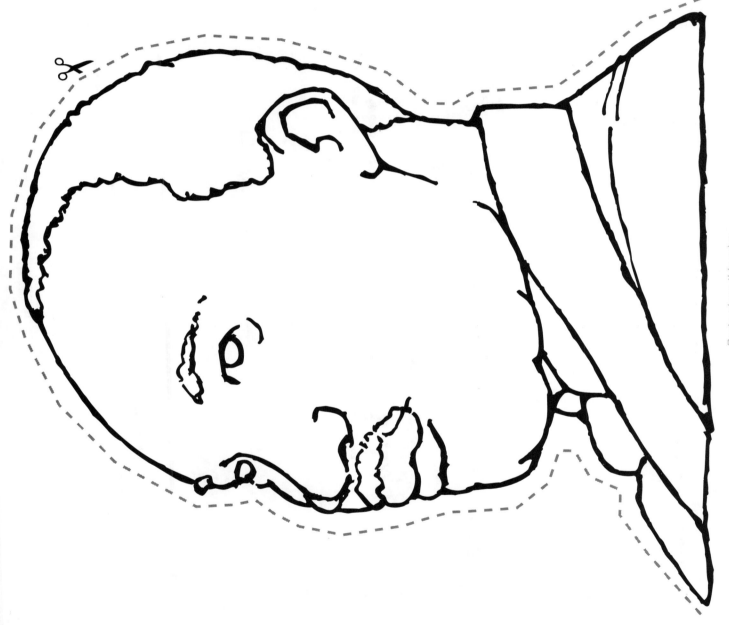

Paste along this edge.

Writing Forms • EMC 596

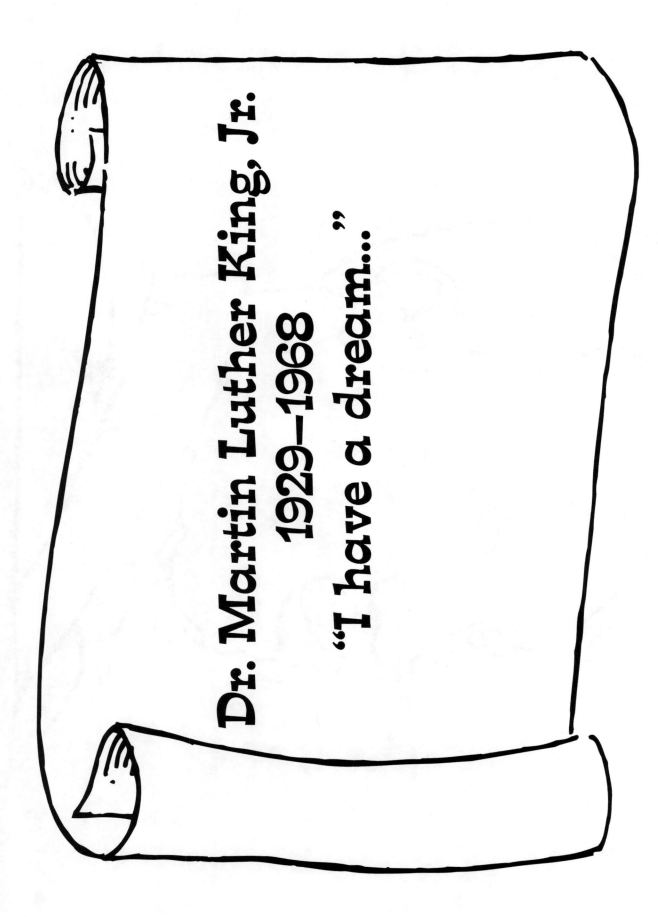

Dr. Martin Luther King, Jr.
1929–1968
"I have a dream..."

Writing Forms • EMC 596

73

Paste along this edge.

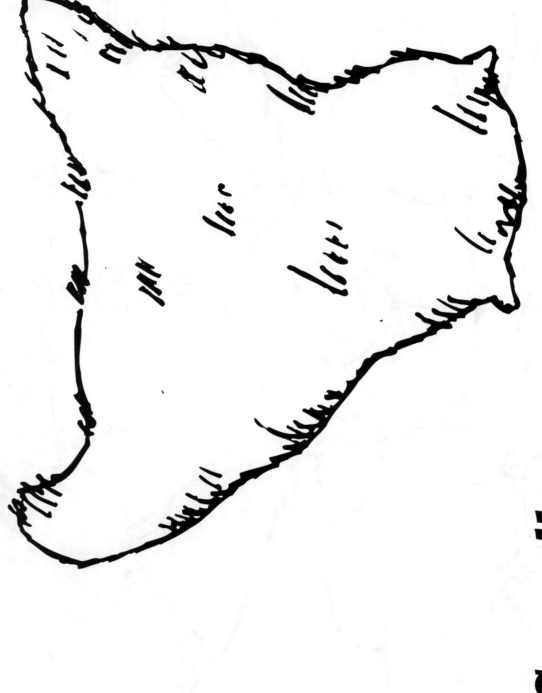

Groundhog

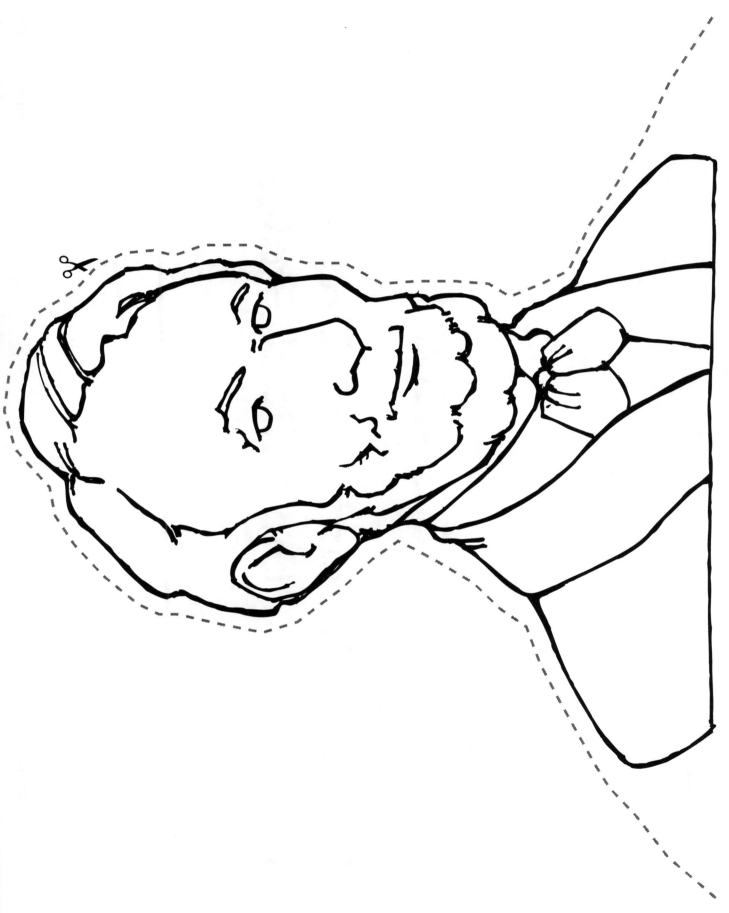

Paste along this edge.

75

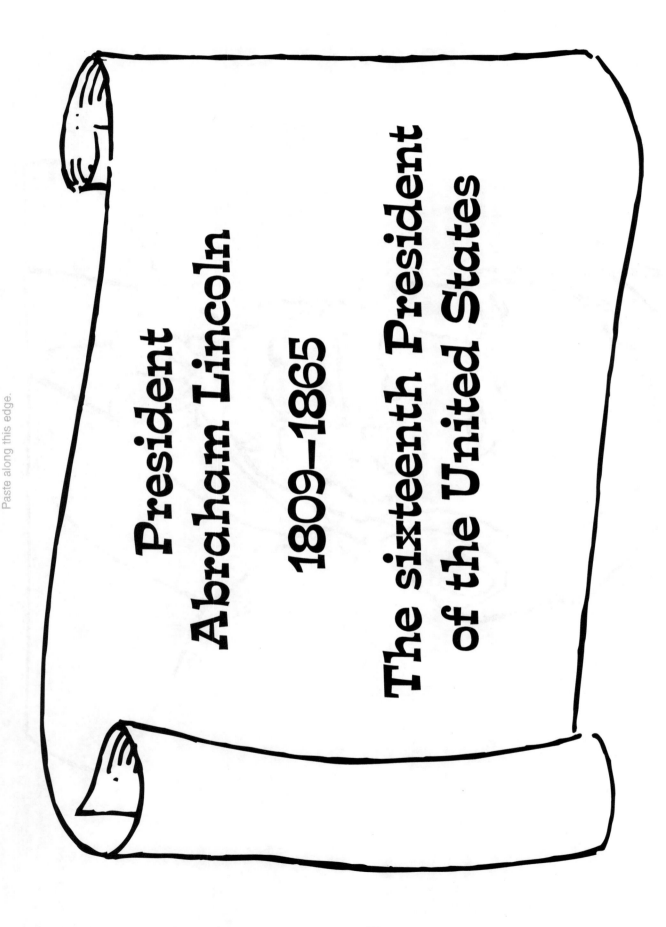

President
Abraham Lincoln

1809–1865

The sixteenth President
of the United States

Writing Forms • EMC 596

Writing Forms • EMC 596

Paste along this edge.

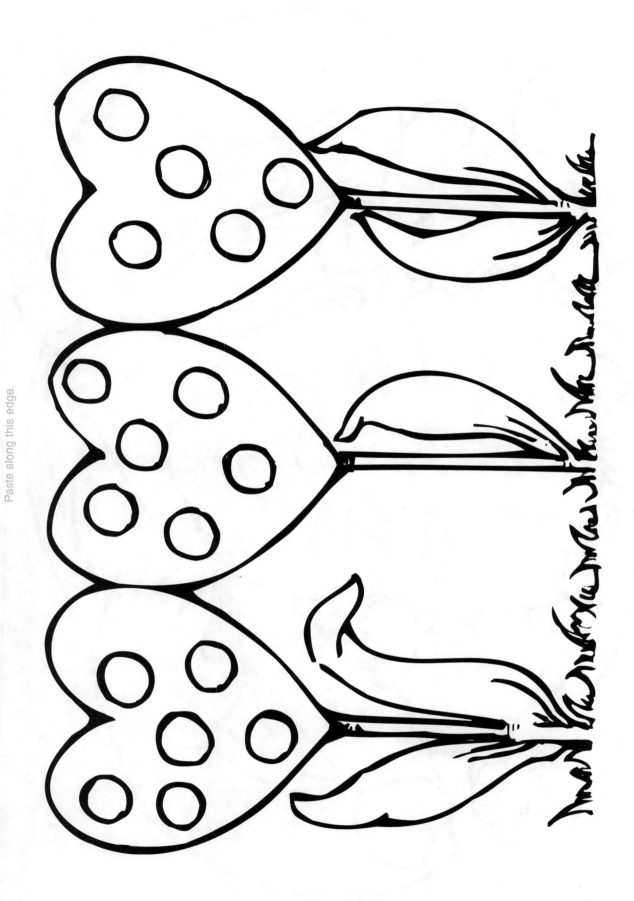

Cupid

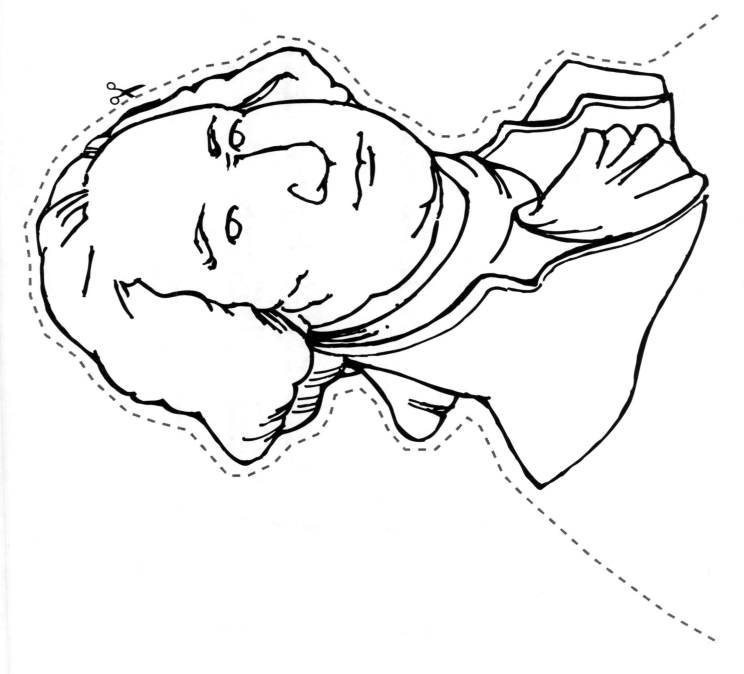

79

Paste along this edge.

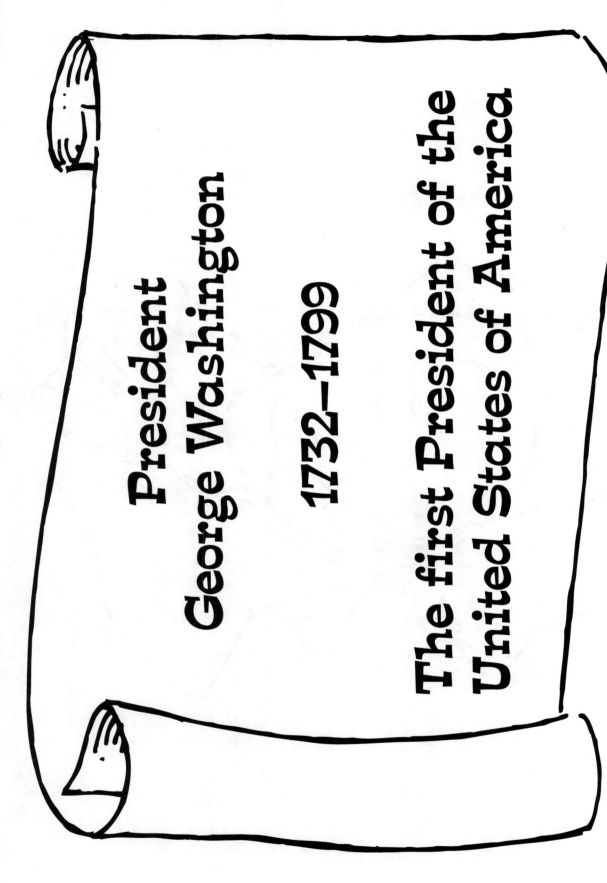

President
George Washington

1732–1799

The first President of the
United States of America

Writing Forms • EMC 596

81

Writing Forms • EMC 596

Paste along this edge.

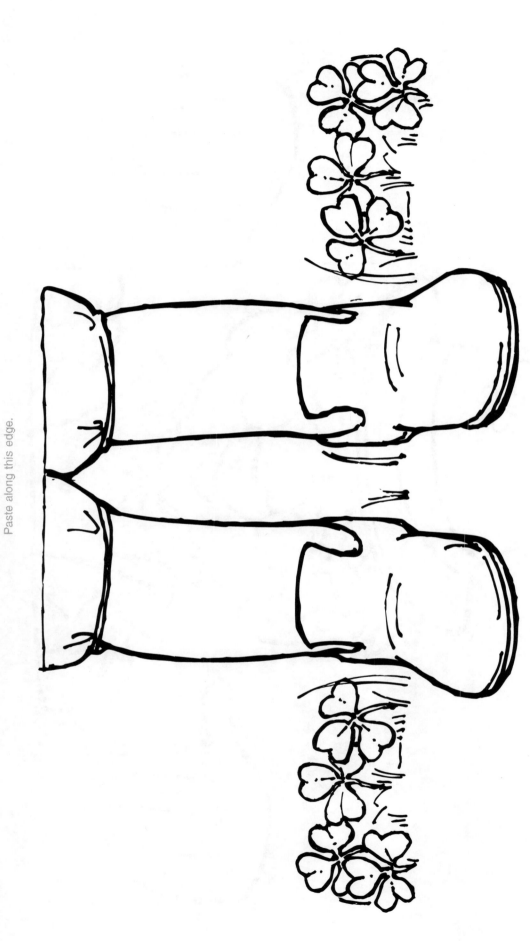

Leprechaun

Writing Forms • EMC 596

Paste along this edge.

Easter Bunny

Writing Forms • EMC 596

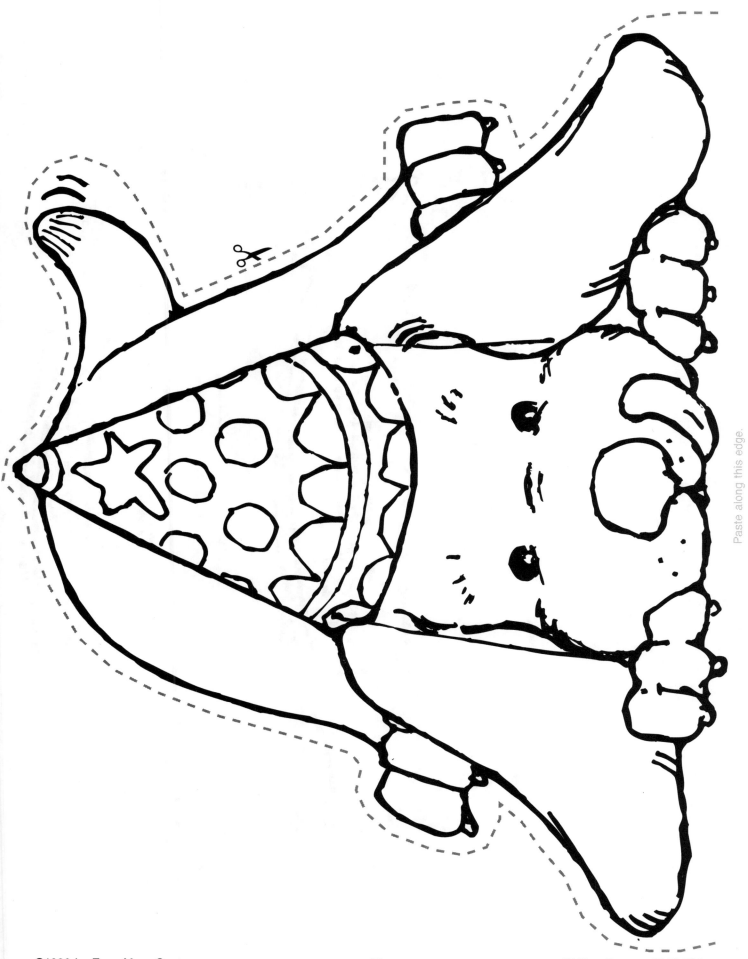

85

Writing Forms • EMC 596

Paste along this edge.

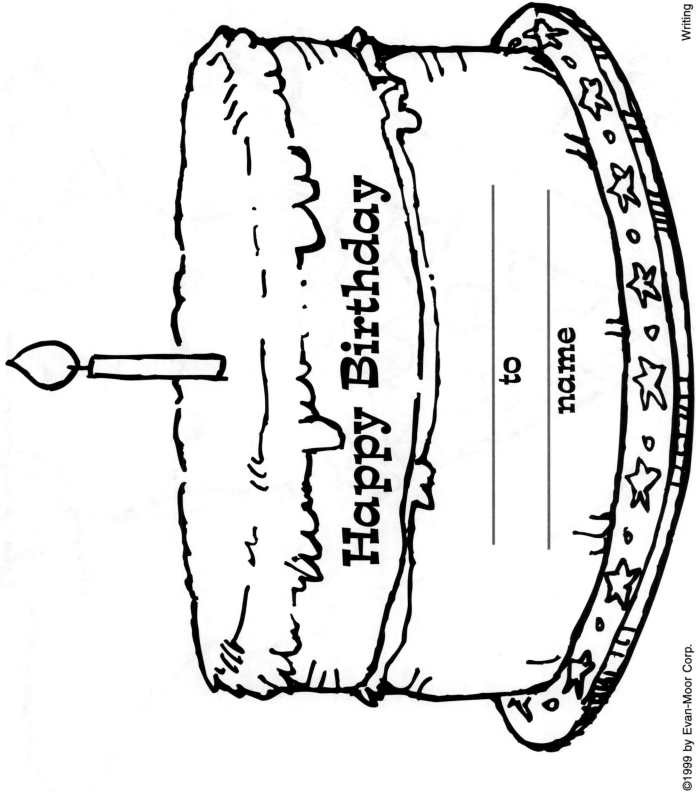

Happy Birthday

to

name

Writing Forms • EMC 596

Children Around the World Writing Forms

Children Around the World writing forms can be used to:

- list facts about the country from which the child comes
- write a descriptive paragraph about what the child is wearing
- write simple reports
- write stories using the child as one of the characters
- copy a favorite poem or create an original poem about the country
- practice handwriting
- create the cover of a class book
- decorate a bulletin board

Cut out the "top."

Paste your own paper to the "top."

Paste the "bottom" to your paper.

An Inuit Girl

Note:

- Children in many parts of the world now wear Western style dress. As you use these forms, it is important to help your students understand that, in most cases, the clothing shown is probably worn only for parties, ceremonies, and festivals. Also help students to understand that our own country is made up of people from all of these countries. Some have been here a long time; others are new arrivals.

- Information is provided on pages 88–92 to share with your students.

An Inuit Girl

The Inuit live in the far north where the land is covered with snow most of the year. They have to dress very warmly because of the cold. The Inuit that live in cities have many kinds of jobs. Most Inuit in villages live by hunting and fishing. They use sleds pulled by huskies or drive snowmobiles.

A Balinese Girl

This girl is learning to be a dancer. She is from the small, beautiful island called Bali. Most families on the island live in villages. They raise gardens and animals to feed their families.

A British Boy

This English boy is wearing his school uniform. England is part of the United Kingdom, which also includes Scotland, Wales, and Northern Ireland. There are large, busy cities and small, quiet villages in England. A game called cricket is the national sport.

A Chinese Girl

China is the second-largest Asian country. The Chinese eat rice, noodles, and other foods using chopsticks instead of a fork and spoon. The Chinese invented many of the things you use such as paper, ink, and writing. Chinese writing uses pictures, not letters.

A Boy from Ecuador

Ecuador is a tiny country in South America. Most people in Ecuador speak Spanish. Although Ecuador is small in area, it has mountains, a rainforest, and long beaches.

A German Boy

Germany is a country in Europe. It has both large cities and farmlands. The boy is wearing leather pants called lederhosen. They are worn for special events.

A Greek Boy

This Greek boy wears the clothing pictured here for special events. Greece is an old country. People have been living there for thousands of years. Most of Greece is close to the sea.

A Hopi Girl

The Hopi are a Native American tribe who live in northern Arizona. Many Hopi are farmers and sheep herders. They also make baskets, pottery, and weave rugs. Other Hopi have jobs such as teachers, police officers, or store clerks.

 Writing Forms • EMC 596

An Indian Boy · **pages 109 and 110**

This Indian boy is dressed for a wedding. India is the third-largest country in Asia. Many different groups of people live in India. They speak many different languages. While there are many large cities, most people still live in the country.

An Irish Girl · **pages 111 and 112**

This girl from Ireland is dressed in her dancing clothes. Ireland is an island divided into two countries. Northern Ireland is part of the United Kingdom. The Republic of Ireland is an independent country. The Irish speak both English and Gaelic. They love music, dancing, and telling stories.

A Japanese Girl · **pages 113 and 114**

This Japanese girl is dressed in a beautiful kimono for a special celebration. Japan is made up of four large islands and many small islands. Japan is mountainous, with little flat land. Crops grow on terraces on the sides of mountains. The Japanese celebrate many holidays.

A Boy from Israel · · · · · · · · · · · · · · · · · · · **pages 115 and 116**

This boy lives in Israel. His hairstyle and clothing show that he is a Hasidic Jew. This group of Jewish people have a special dress code. Jews from all over the world now live in Israel.

A Saami Boy

This Saami boy wears traditional brightly colored warm clothing. It is very cold much of the time where he lives above the Arctic Circle. Some Saami still travel from place to place with their reindeer herds. They use reindeer for food, clothing, and to pull sleds. Today, most Saami have other ways to earn a living and live in modern towns.

A Masai Girl

She is wearing bright jewelry and has her head shaved. This is the custom of her people, a group called the Masai. The Masai live in the African countries of Tanzania and Kenya. Most Masai live in villages and raise herds of cattle.

A Mexican Boy

This Mexican boy is dressed to ride in a rodeo. Mexico is a large country in North America. There are large modern cities and small villages in Mexico. The people speak Spanish. Tomato, crocodile, tornado, and cafeteria are some of the words we use that come from the Spanish language.

A Girl from Nigeria

This girl belongs to a group of people called the Yoruba. The Yoruba live in the African country of Nigeria. The Yoruba may live in cities or in villages. In the villages, several families will live in an area called a compound. They farm the land.

A Boy from Oman

This boy is from a small country on the Arabian Peninsula called Oman. Most people in Oman speak Arabic. Boys and girls study the same subjects, but they go to different schools.

A Russian Girl

This girl is from Russia. Russia is a very large country. Part of Russia is in Europe and part is in Asia. It has high mountains, grassy plains, hot deserts, and frozen lands. Russia has both modern cities and small farming villages. The Russian people love music, poetry, and stories.

A Samoan Boy

This boy lives on one of the Samoan Islands in the Pacific Ocean. His festival dress is called a "lavalava." There will be food, dancing, games, and contests at the festival.

A Sherpa Girl

This girl is a Sherpa. The Sherpa live high up in the Himalaya mountains where they farm and raise animals. They trade at outdoor markets for the goods the family needs. They use yaks, a kind of cattle, for transportation and for food.

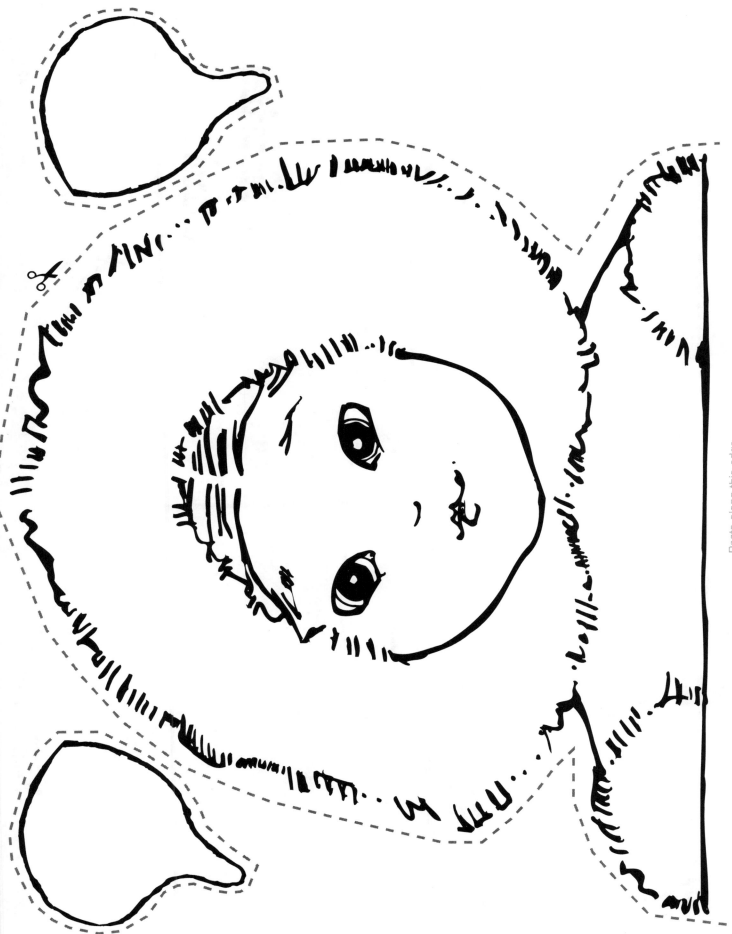

Paste along this edge

An Inuit Girl

Writing Forms • EMC 596

Paste along this edge.

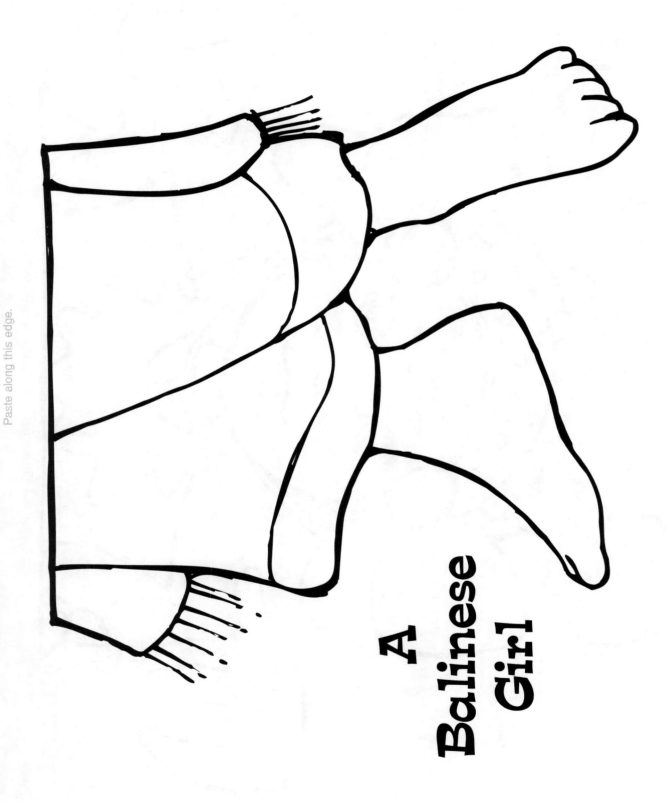

A Balinese Girl

Writing Forms • EMC 596

Paste along this edge.

97

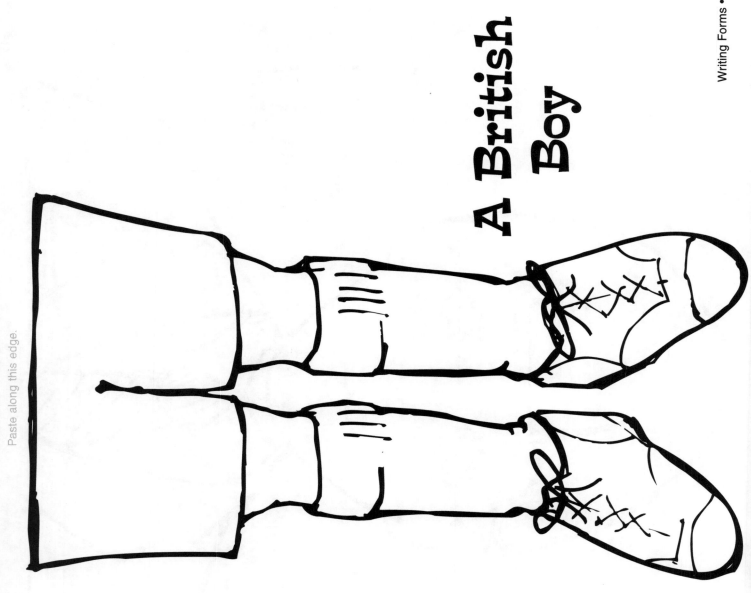

A British Boy

Writing Forms • EMC 596

Writing Forms • EMC 596

Paste along this edge.

A Chinese Girl

Writing Forms • EMC 596

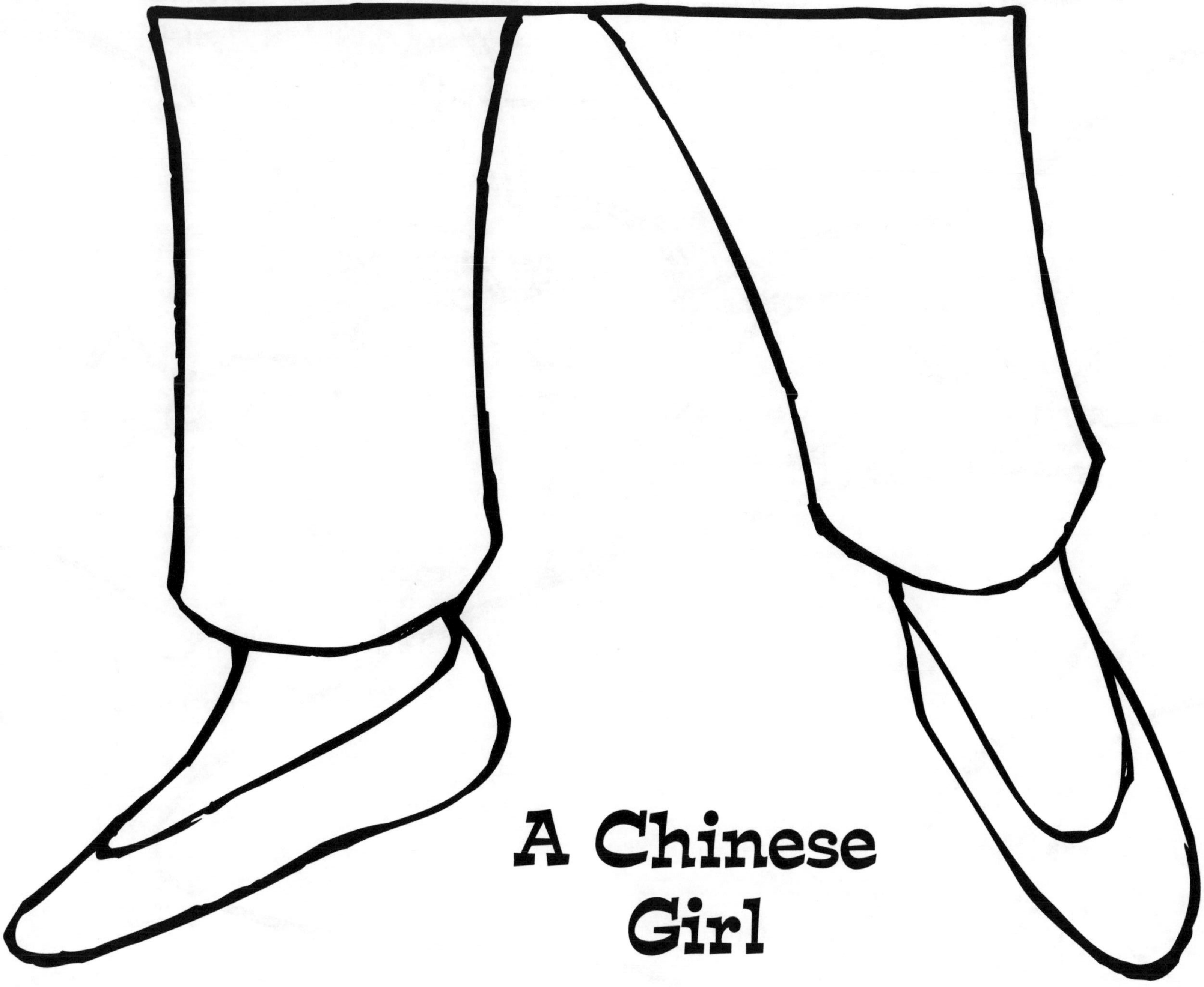

Paste along this edge.

101

Paste along this edge.

A Boy from Ecuador

Paste along this edge.

Writing Forms • EMC 596

A German Boy

Paste along this edge.

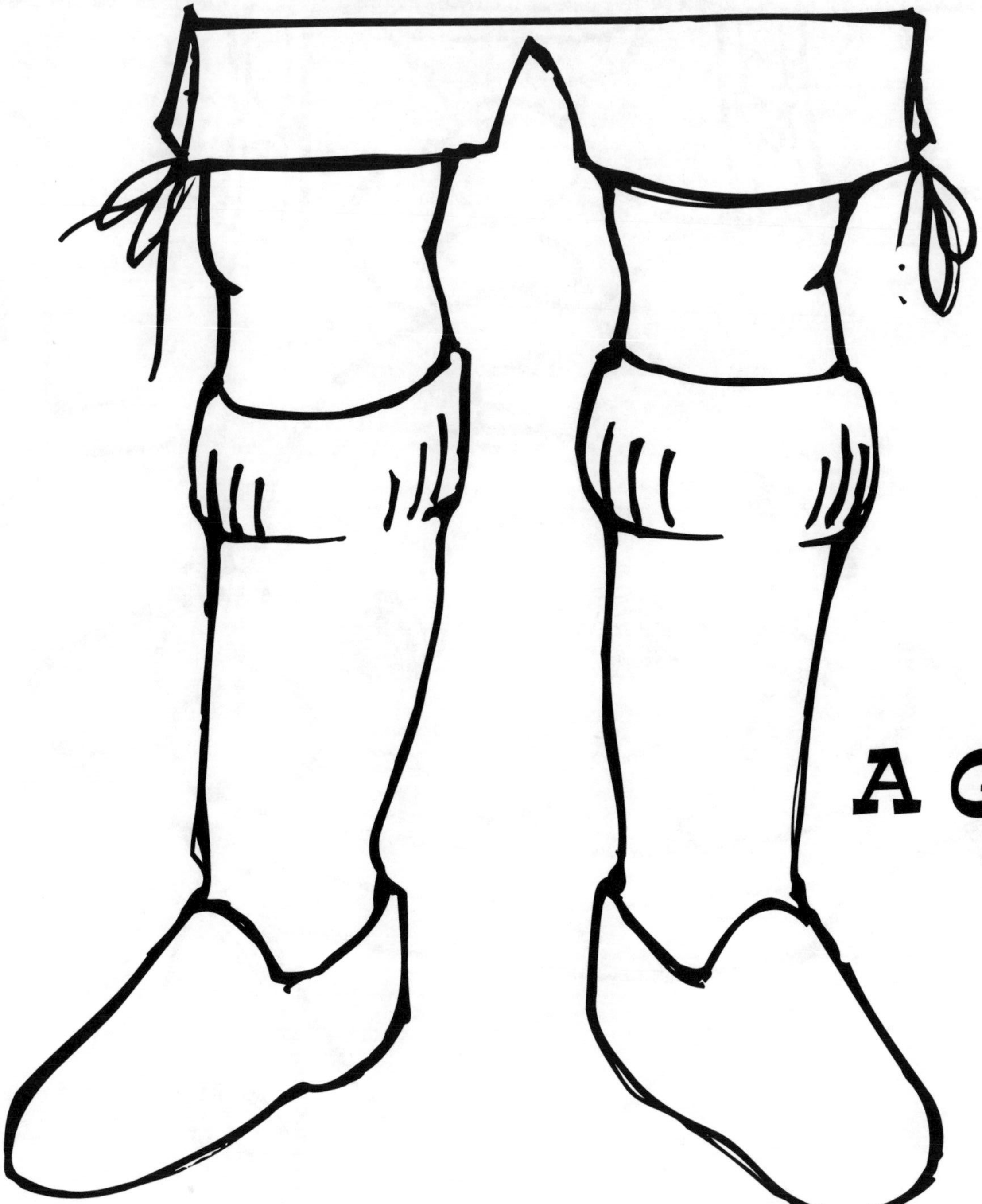

Writing Forms • EMC 596

Paste along this edge.

Writing Forms • EMC 596

A Greek
Boy

Writing Forms • EMC 596

Writing Forms • EMC 596

Paste along this edge.

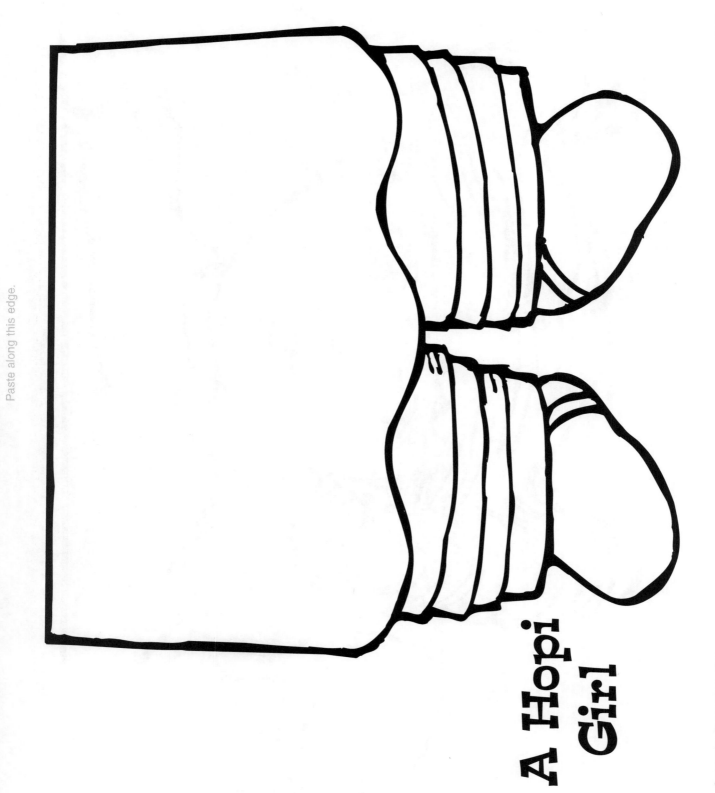

A Hopi Girl

Paste along this edge.

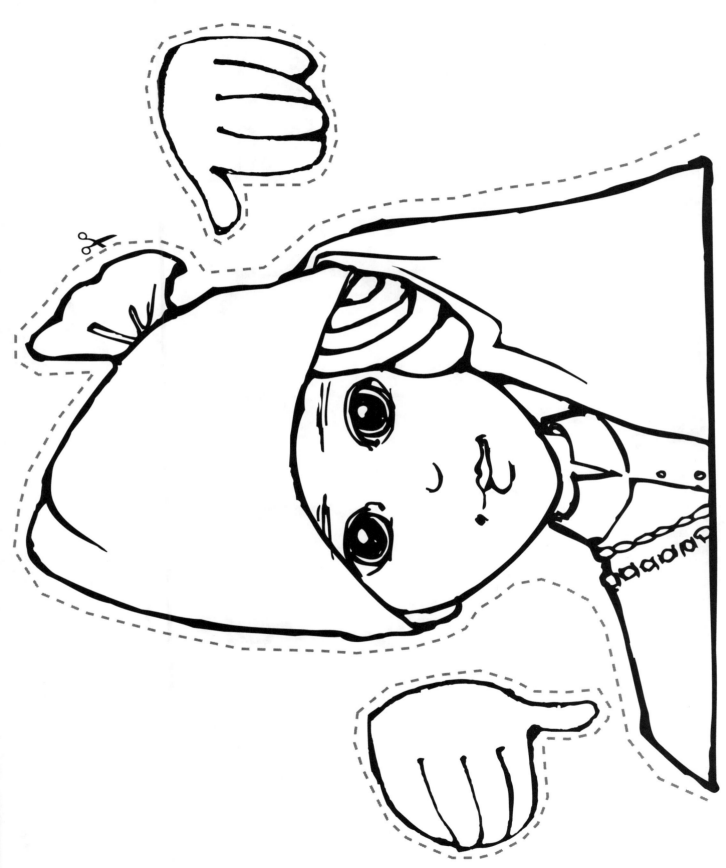

Paste along this edge.

109

An Indian Boy

Writing Forms • EMC 596

Paste along this edge.

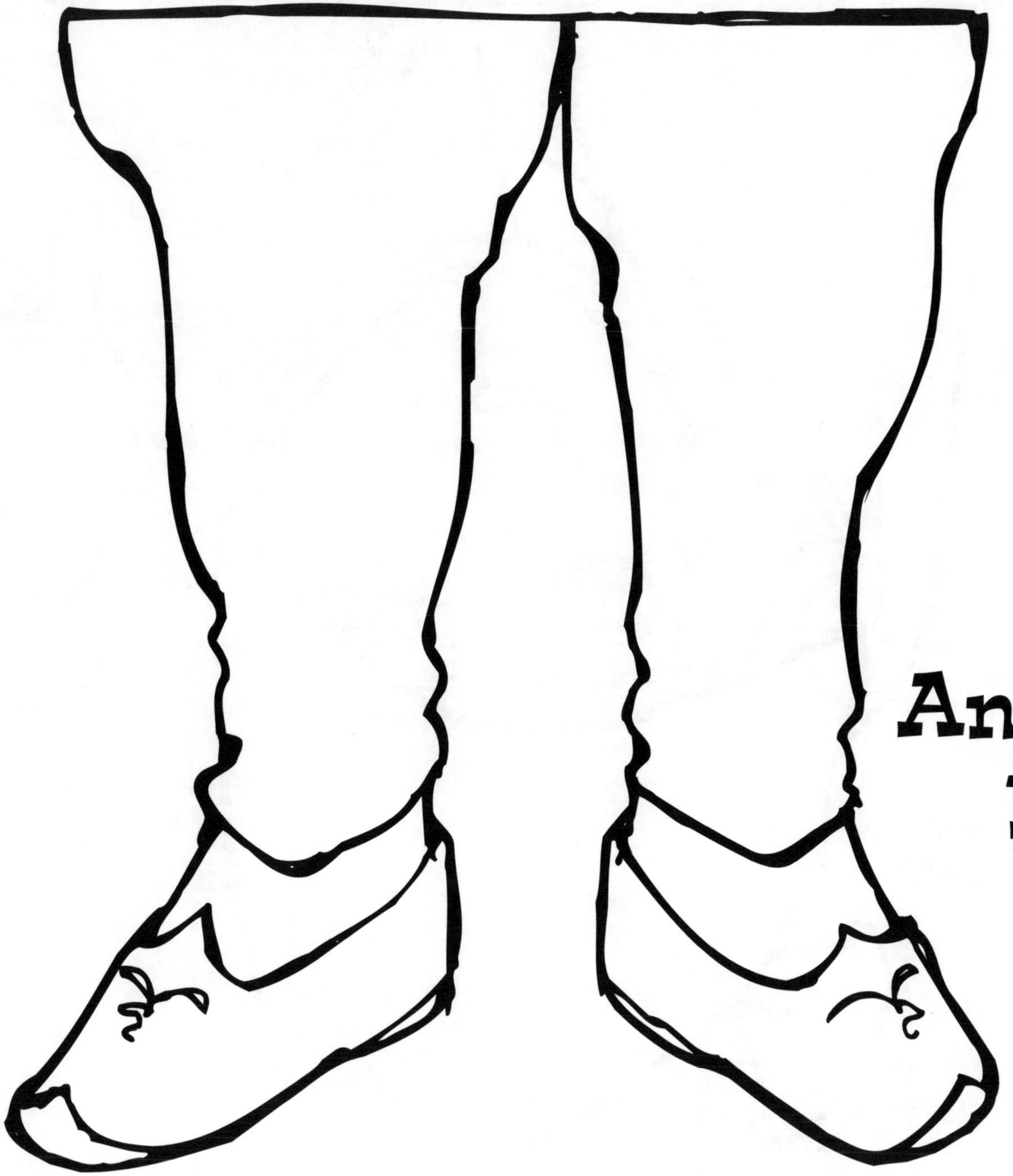

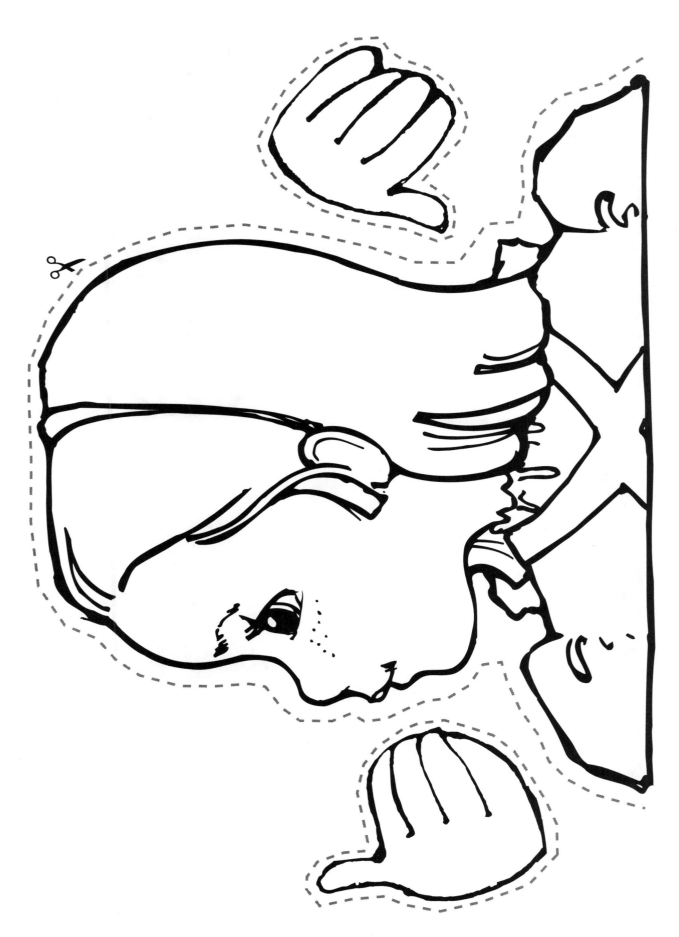

Paste along this edge.

Writing Forms • EMC 596

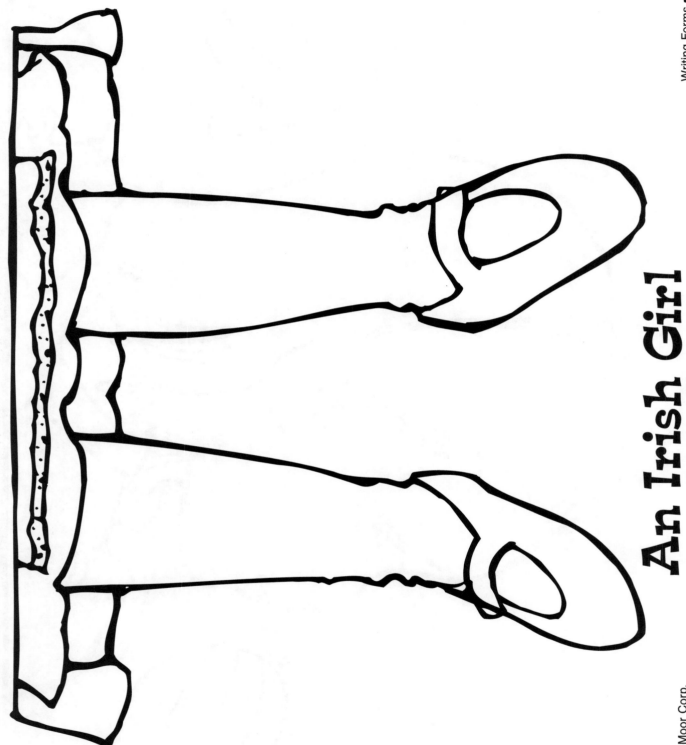

An Irish Girl

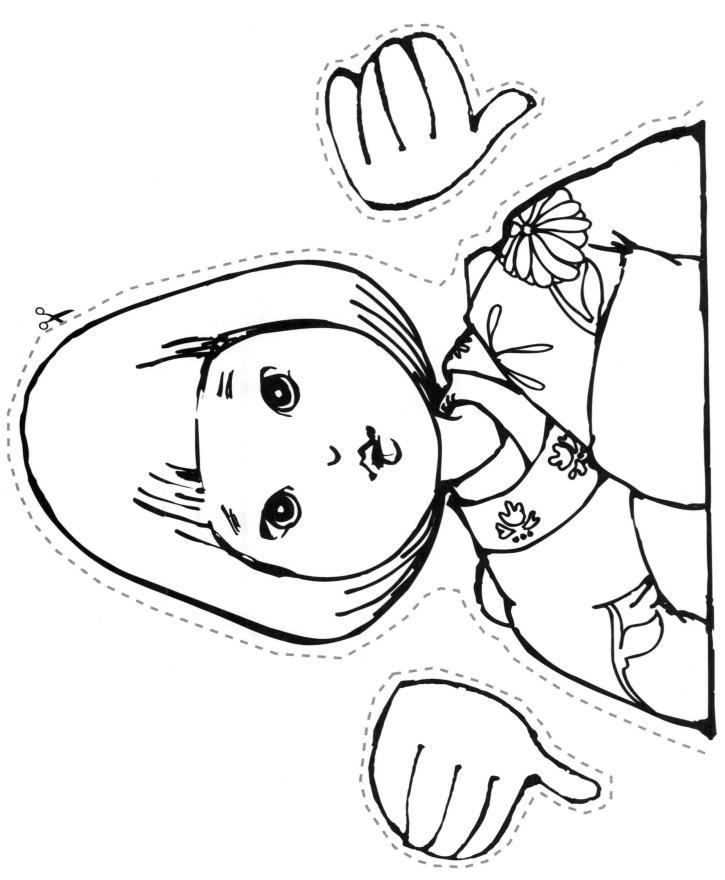

113

Paste along this edge.

A Japanese Girl

Writing Forms • EMC 596

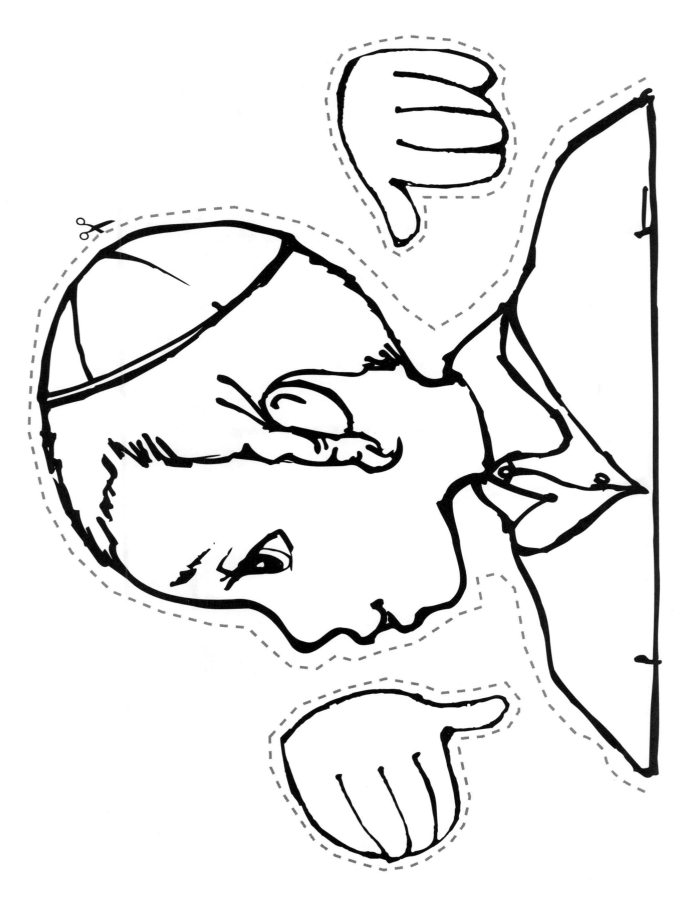

Paste along this edge.

115

A Boy from Israel

Writing Forms • EMC 596

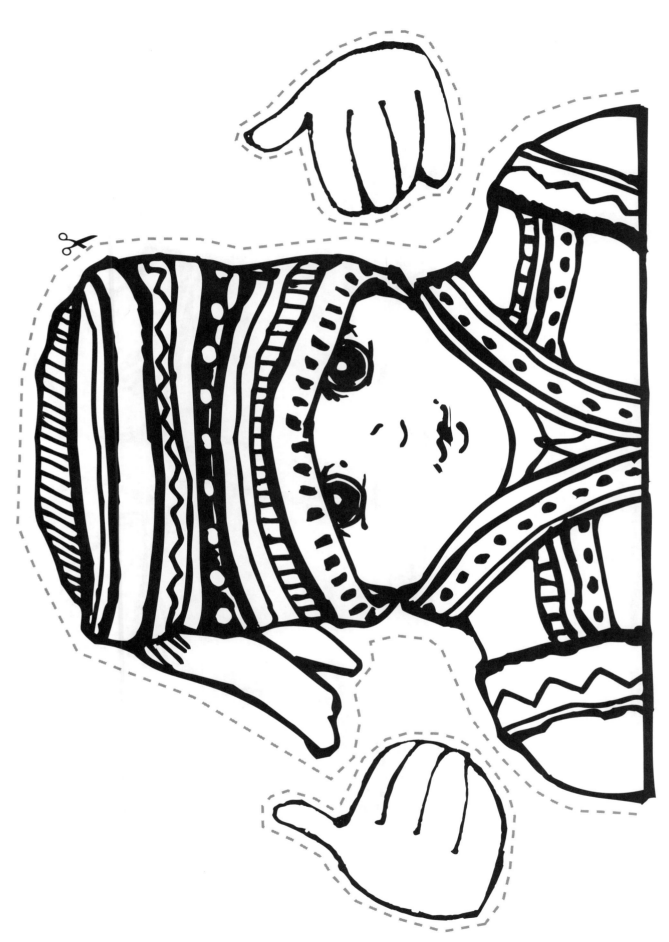

117

Paste along this edge.

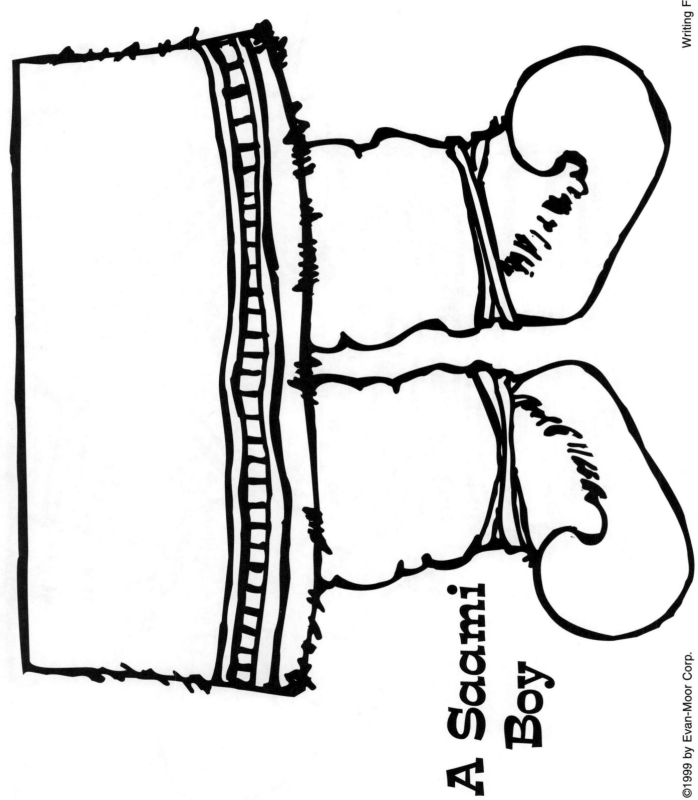

A Saami Boy

Paste along this edge.

Writing Forms • EMC 596

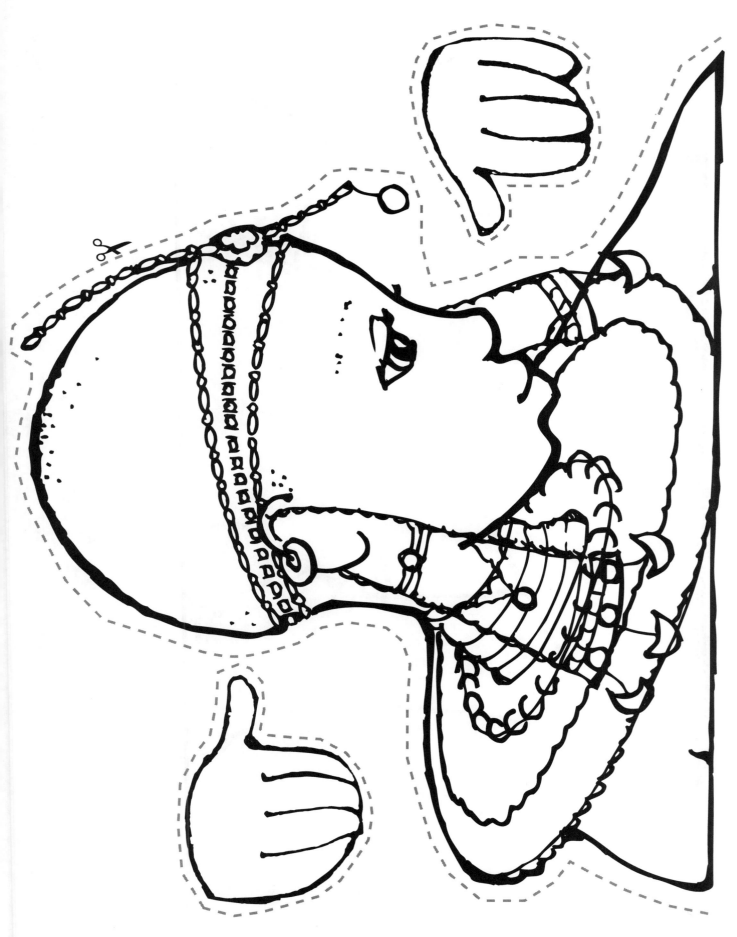

119

Paste along this edge.

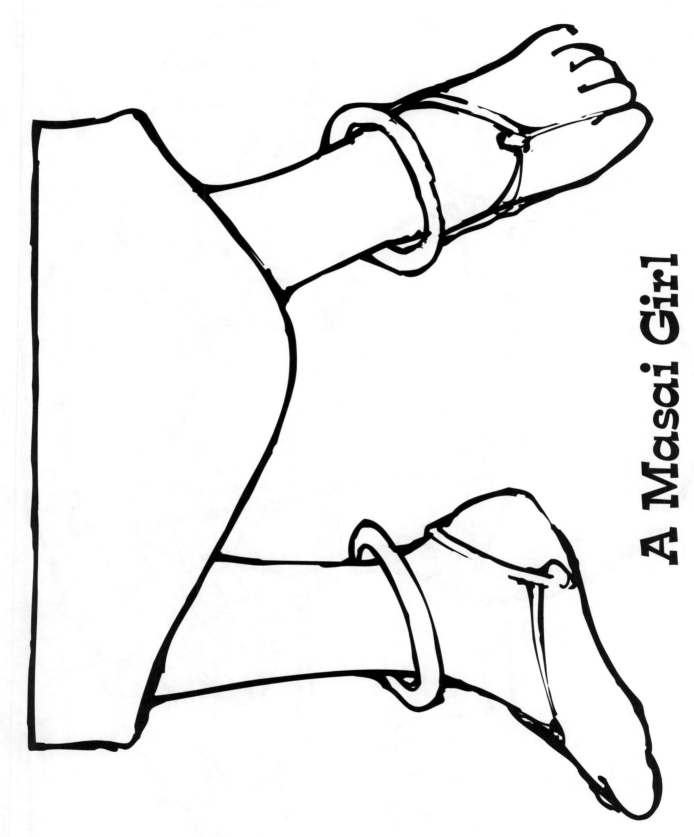

Writing Forms • EMC 596

A Masai Girl

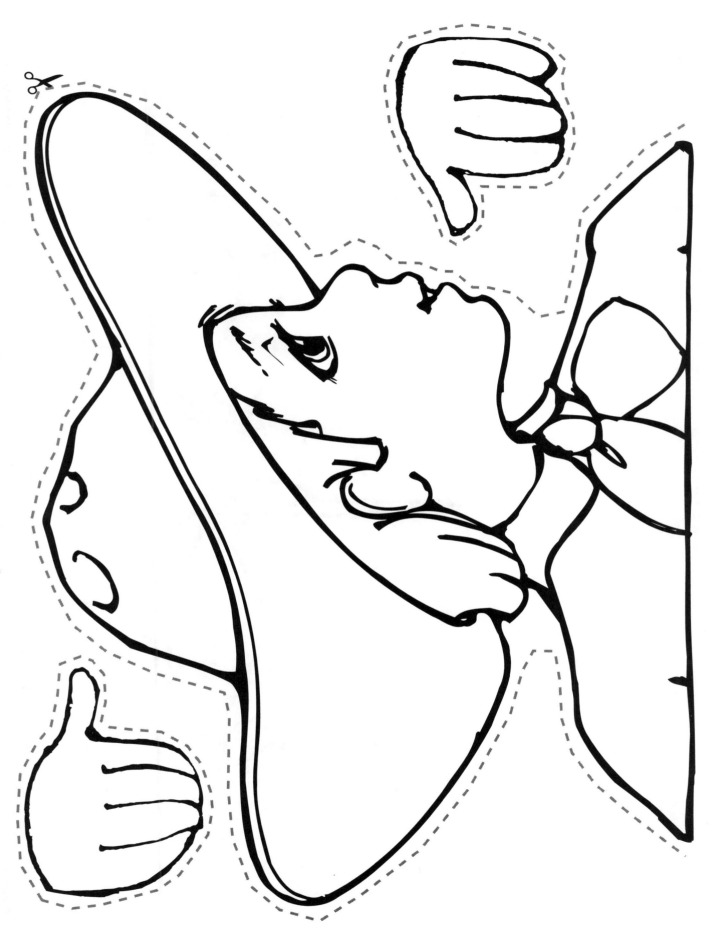

121

Paste along this edge.

A Mexican Boy

Paste along this edge.

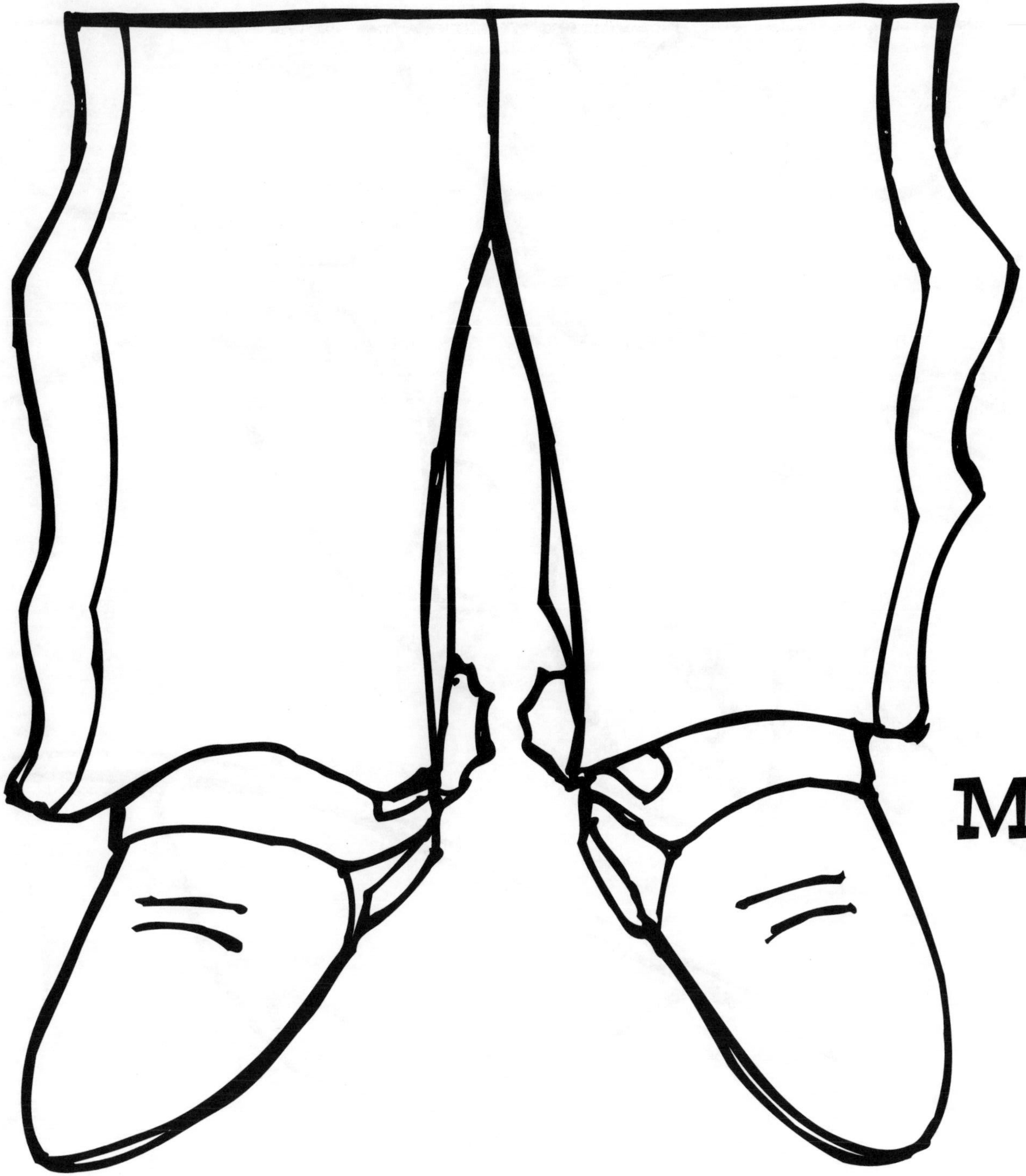

Writing Forms • EMC 596

Paste along this edge.

Writing Forms • EMC 596

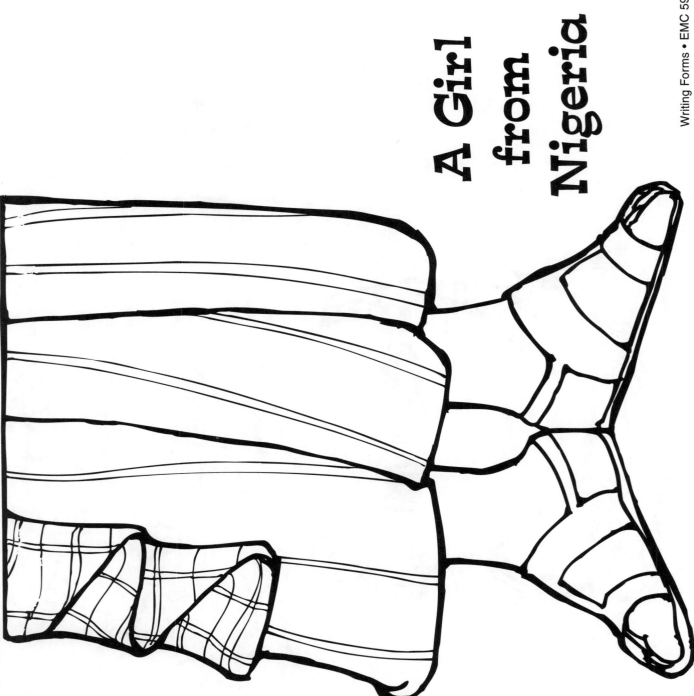

A Girl from Nigeria

Writing Forms • EMC 596

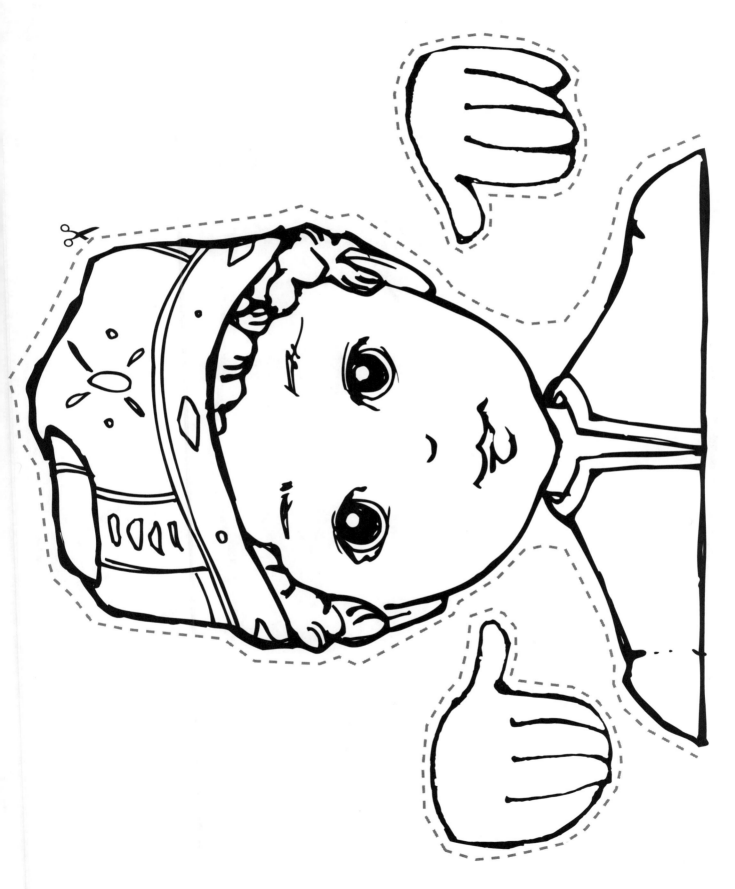

125

Paste along this edge.

Paste along this edge.

A Boy from Oman

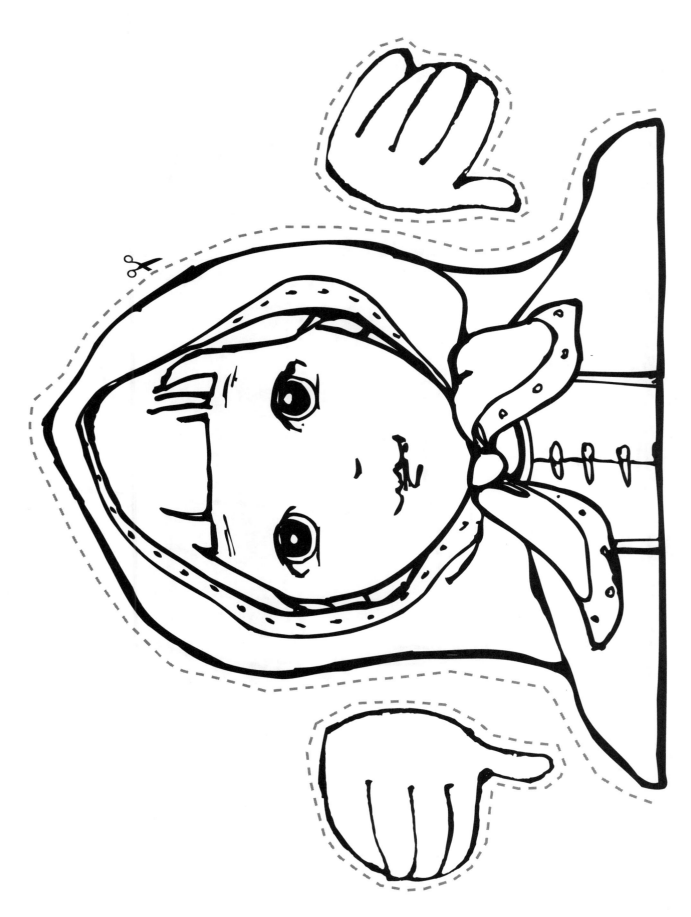

Paste along this edge.

Writing Forms • EMC 596

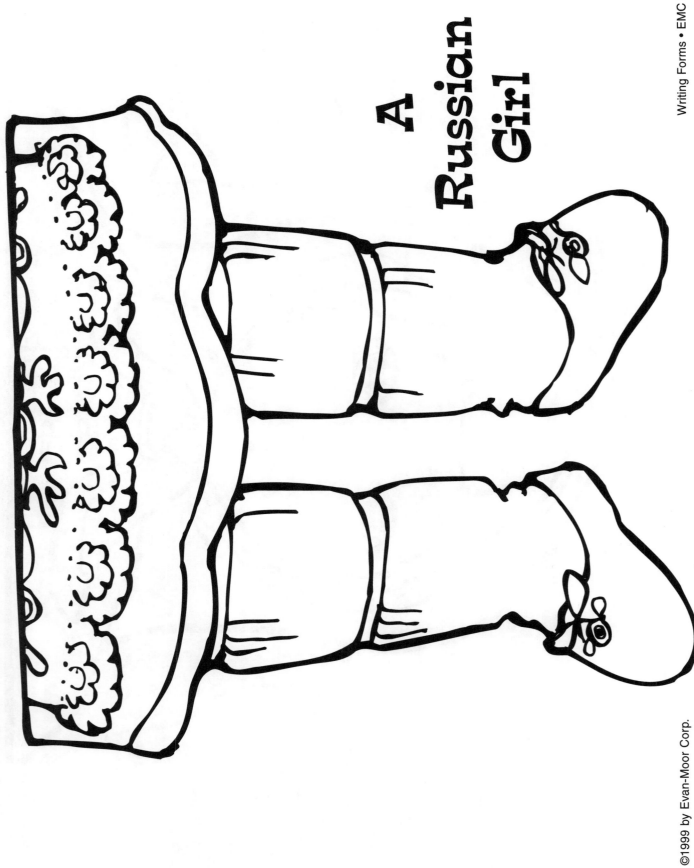

A Russian Girl

Writing Forms • EMC 596

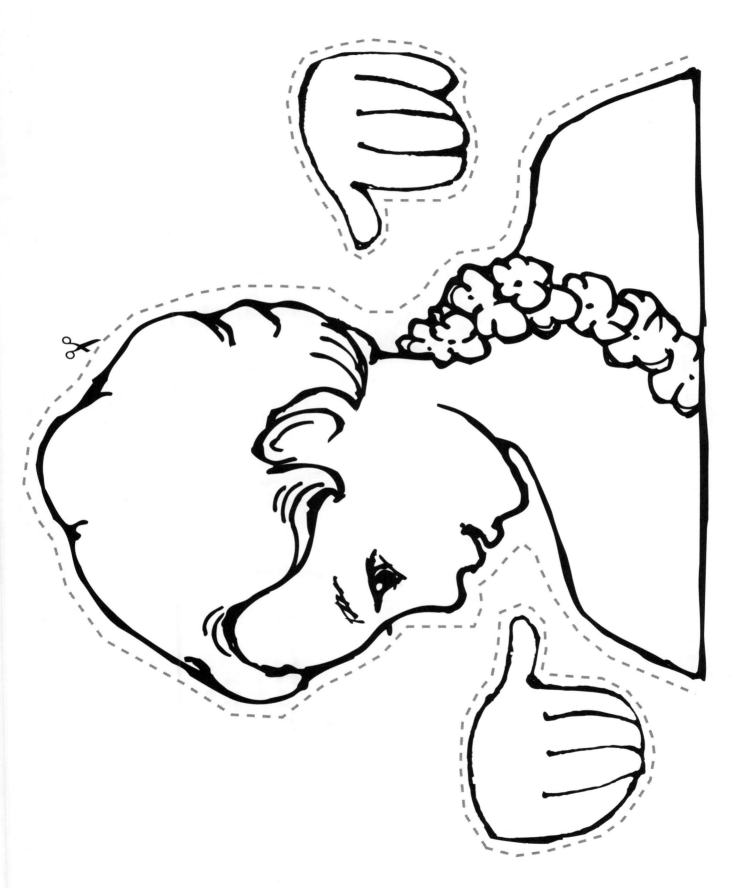

Paste along this edge.

129

A
Samoan
Boy

131

Paste along this edge.

Writing Forms • EMC 596

A Sherpa Girl

People at Work Writing Forms

People at Work writing forms can be used to:

- list facts about the worker
- list the equipment used by the worker and describe how it is used
- write simple reports about what the worker does
- write stories about an event or day in the life of the worker
- copy poems or write original poems about the worker
- practice handwriting
- display student work on a bulletin board
- decorate a bulletin board

Pages 134–136 provide an overview of the People at Work writing forms. For each occupation, there are two story starters and a word list. Put the word list on a large chart or on the chalkboard for students to refer to when writing about that worker.

Cut out the "top."

Paste your own paper to the "top."

Paste the "bottom" to your paper.

Bus
Driver

Fire Fighter .... pages 137 and 138

fire engine	ladder truck	hose
nozzle	ladder	helmet
rubber boots	face mask	horn
hatchet	fire hydrant	oxygen tank
fire extinguisher	fire	rescue

Story starters:

The fire engine raced to the fire....
If I were a fire fighter....

Mail Carrier .... pages 139 and 140

mail pouch	deliver	stamps
letters	mail truck	route
postcards	packages	mailbox

Story starters:

"What is that strange sound in my mail pouch?" asked the mail carrier.
If I were a mail carrier....

Teacher .... pages 141 and 142

school	chalkboard	teach
students	children	desk
book	classroom	recess
school bus	field trip	storytime
math	science	reading

Story starters:

My teacher is sick. Who will teach us today?
If I were a teacher....

Police Officer .... pages 143 and 144

uniform	badge	police dog
siren	squad car	criminal
search	chase	victim
help	rescue	protect

Story starters:

The lights flashed as the police car hurried to....
If I were a police officer....

Carpenter · **pages 145 and 146**

toolbox	hammer	repair
saw	lumber	build
screwdriver	nails	fix
measuring tape	plans	tool belt

Story starters:

"I think I'll build a _____ today," said the carpenter.
If I were a carpenter....

Doctor · **pages 147 and 148**

office	x-ray	nurse
help	germs	stethoscope
examine	infection	disease
sick	prescription	hospital

Story starters:

"Where does it hurt?" asked Dr. Jenkins.
If I were a doctor....

Scientist · **pages 149 and 150**

lab	problem	test
measure	study	examine
microscope	experiment	test tube
discover	notes	wonder

Story starters:

"I just discovered _____!" shouted the scientist.
If I were a scientist....

Musician · · · · · · · · · · · · · · · · · · · **pages 151 and 152**

instrument	practice	music
play	music stand	rehearse
compose	orchestra	band
singer	keyboard	drums
horn	piano	guitar

Story starters:

The musicians were surprised to find....
If I were a musician....

Office Worker · pages 153 and 154

desk	telephone	intercom
file cabinet	computer	mail
memo	meeting	calendar
copy machine	stapler	letter opener
in-box	out-box	pager

Story starters:

It's been a busy morning at the office. First....
If I worked in an office....

Bus Driver · pages 155 and 156

bus	bus stop	route
passenger	bus pass	fare
drive	stop	brake
steps	door	emergency exit

Story starters:

Today I'm going to ride the bus to _____.
If I were a bus driver....

Dentist · pages 157 and 158

drill	examine	clean teeth
braces	x-ray	fill cavities
assistant	office	fluoride
toothbrush	toothpaste	floss

Story starters:

"Open wide," said the dentist. "I need to _____."
If I were a dentist....

Farmer · pages 159 and 160

farm	ranch	orchard
barn	shed	silo
dairy	crops	herd
flock	tractor	pickup truck
pasture	corral	plow
combine	plant	harvest

Story starters:

Someone left the barn door open and....
If I were a farmer....

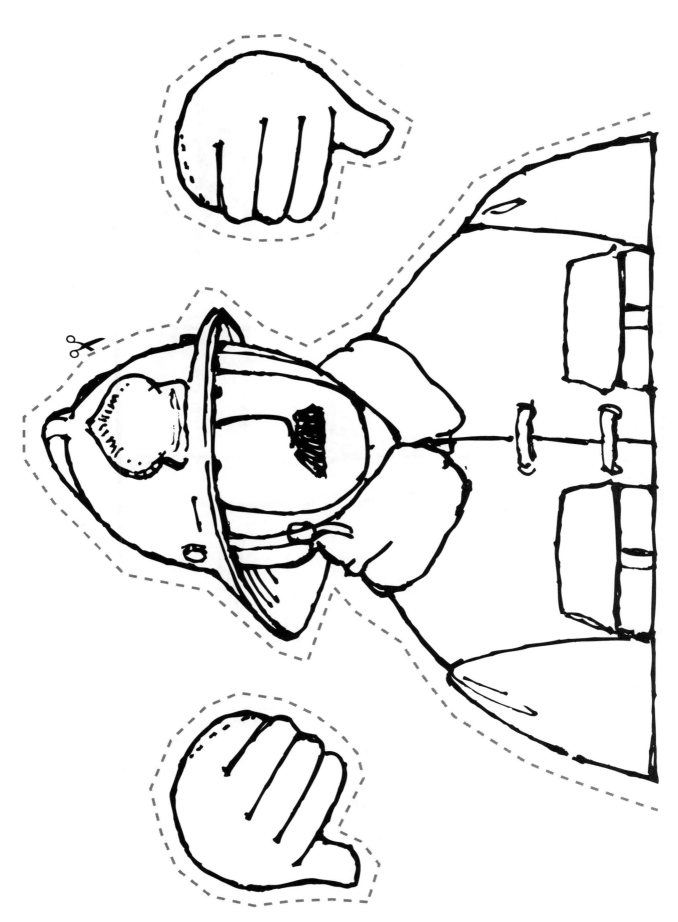

137

Paste along this edge

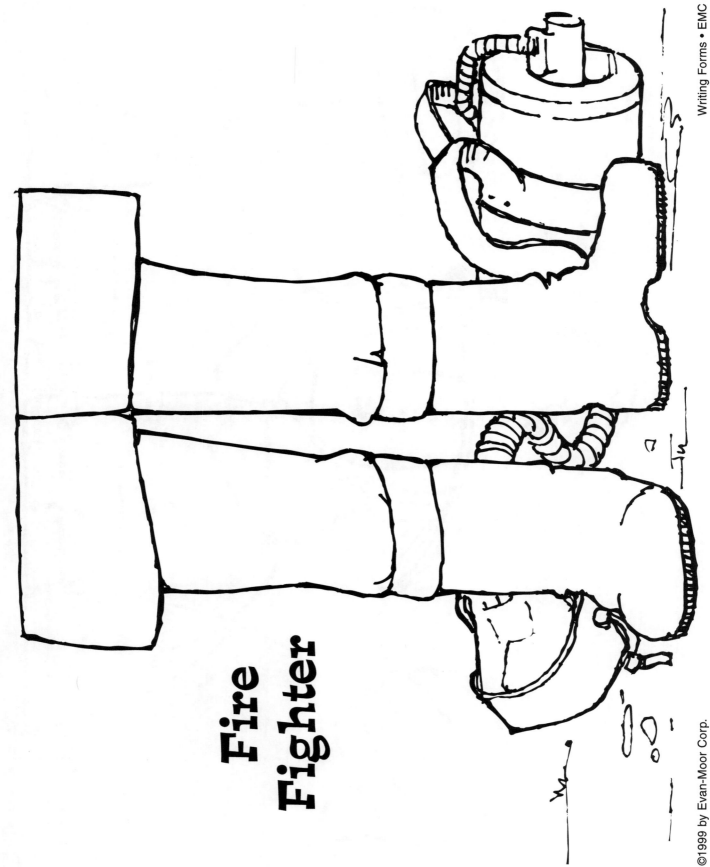

Fire Fighter

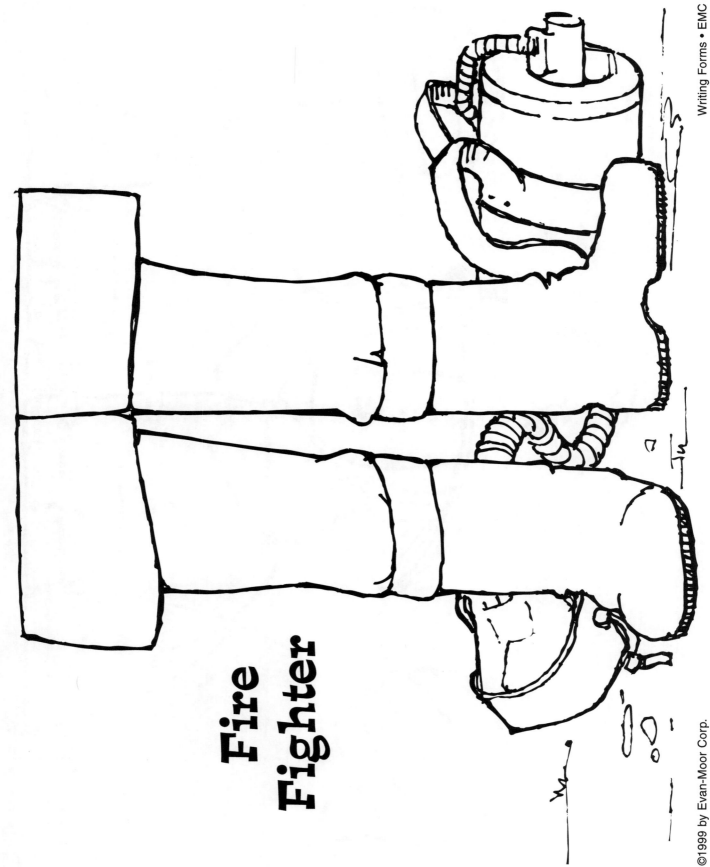

Paste along this edge.

Writing Forms • EMC 596

©1999 by Evan-Moor Corp.

138

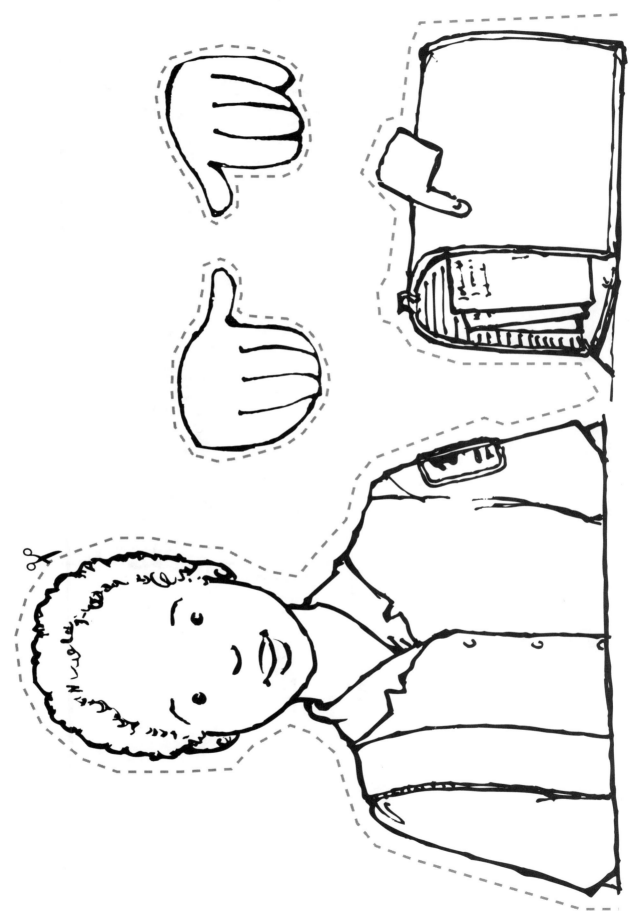

Paste along this edge.

139

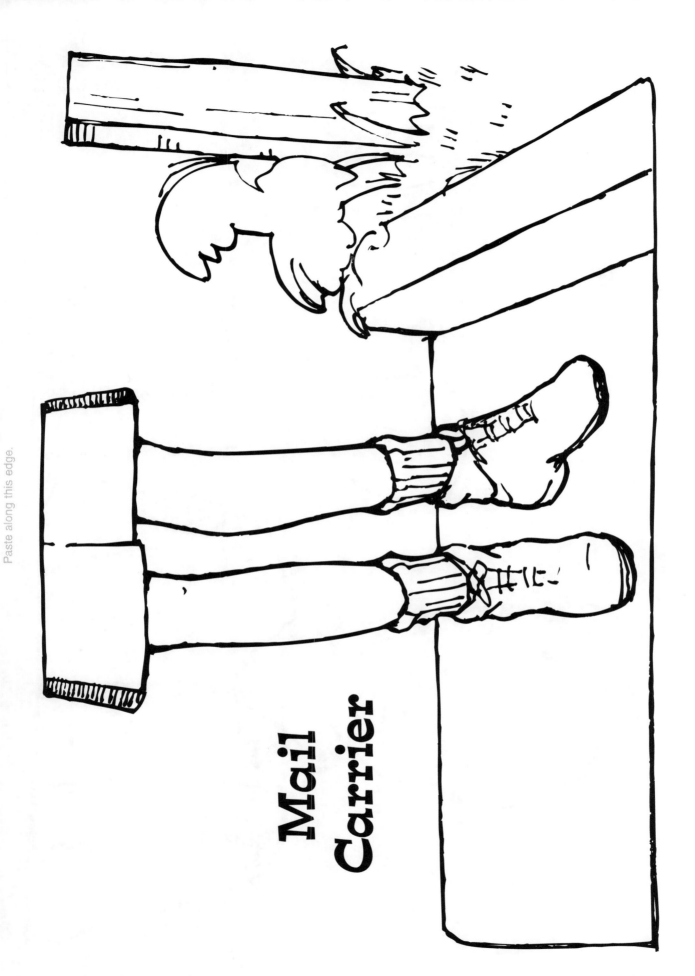

Mail Carrier

Writing Forms • EMC 596

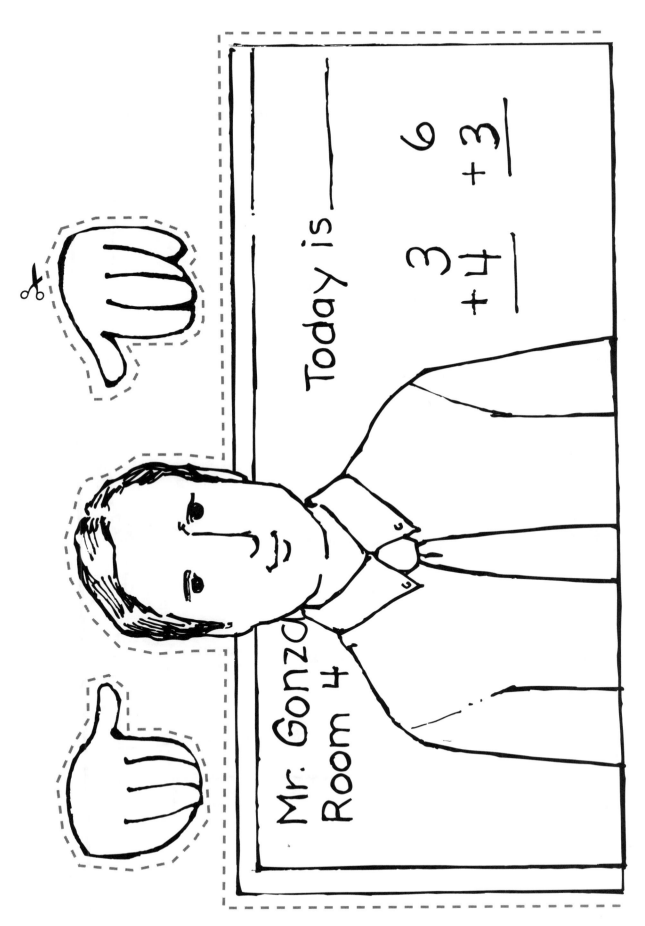

Today is _____

3   6
+4 +3
___ ___

Mr. Gonzo
Room 4

Paste along this edge.

Writing Forms • EMC 596

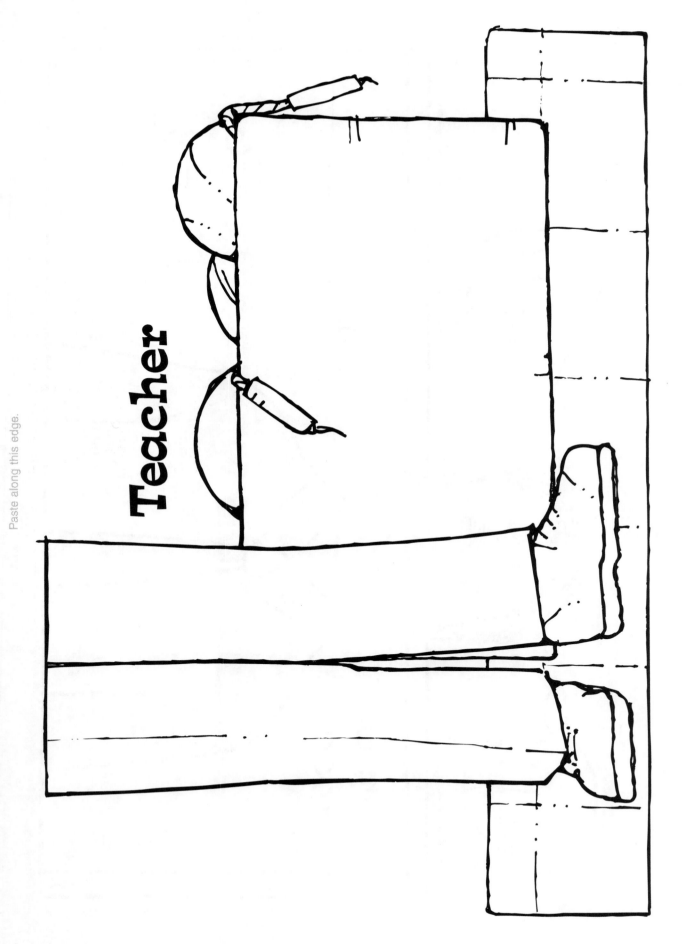

Teacher

Writing Forms • EMC 596

Writing Forms • EMC 596

Paste along this edge.

Police Officer

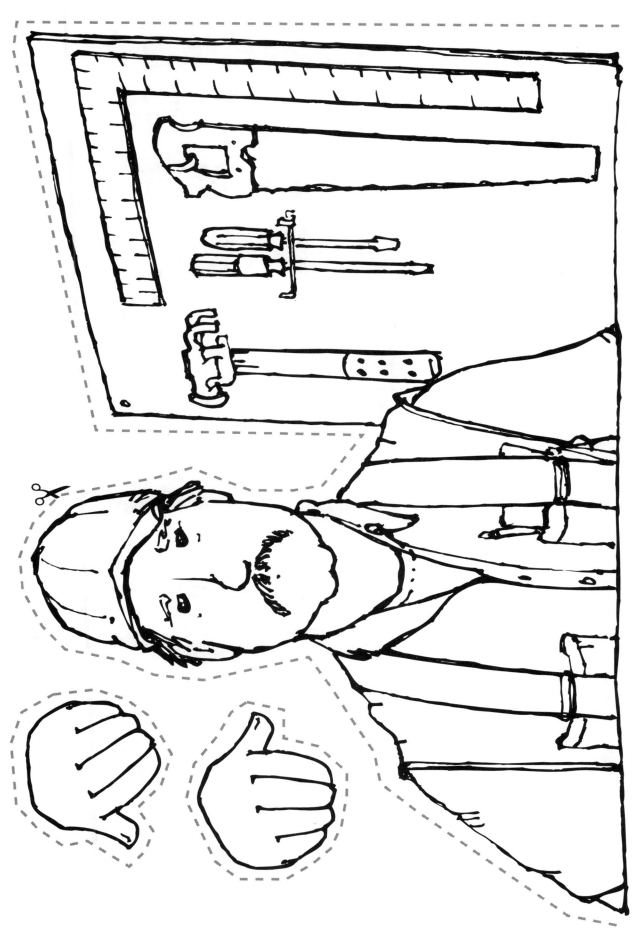

145

Paste along this edge.

Carpenter

Writing Forms • EMC 596

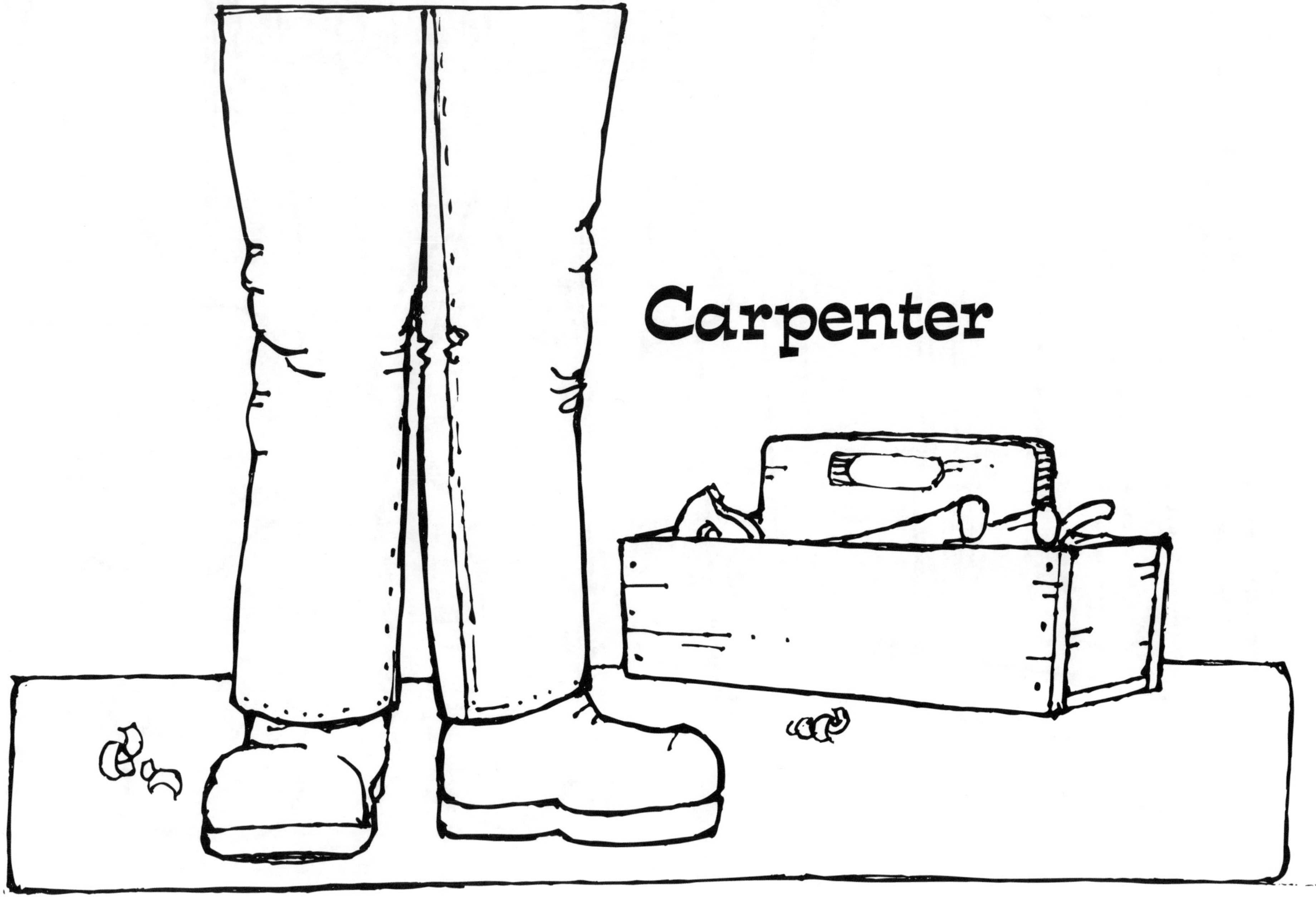

Diploma
Pediatrician

Dr Brown

DR. Brown

Paste along this edge.

Doctor

Writing Forms • EMC 596

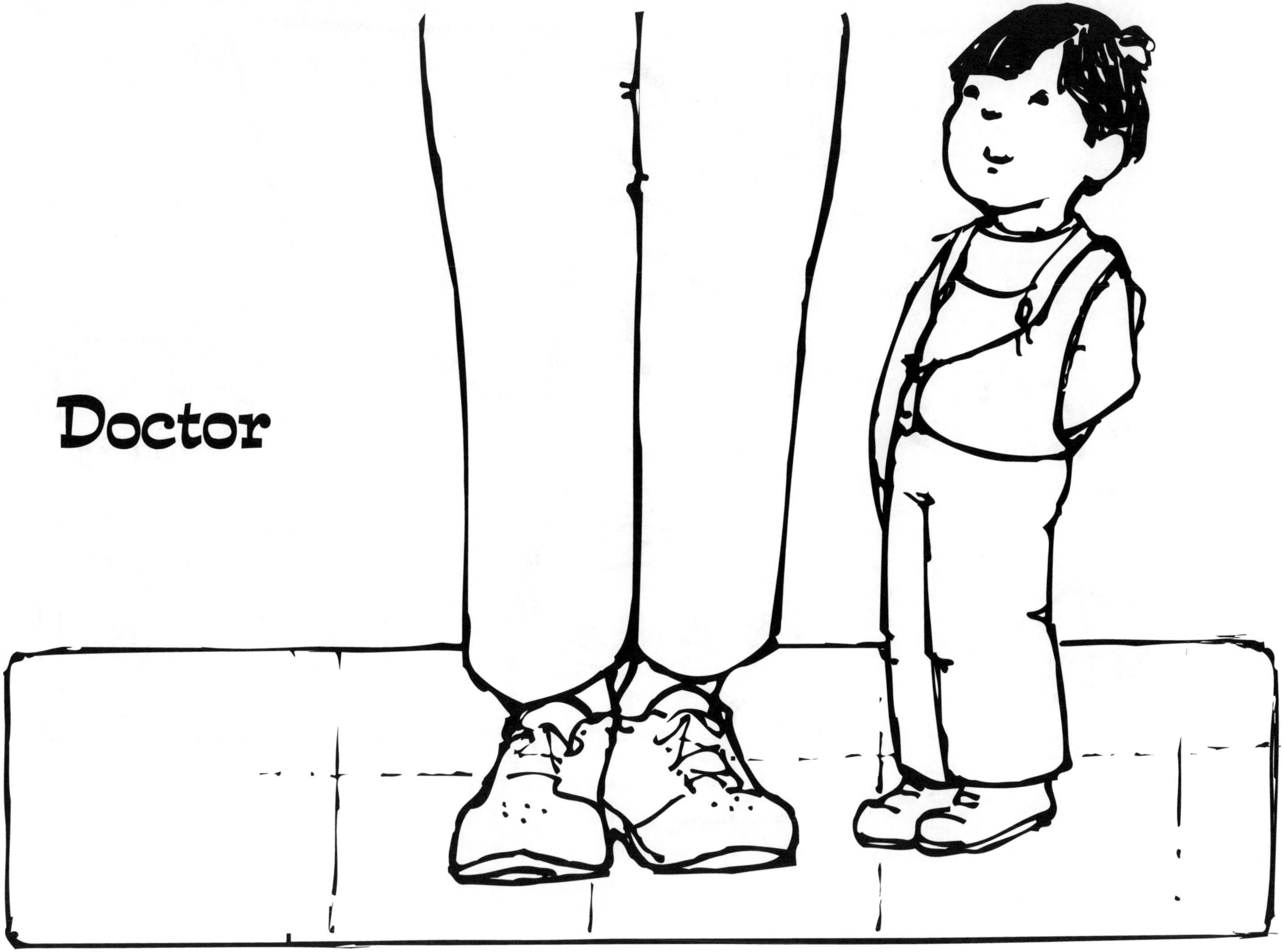

Paste along this edge.

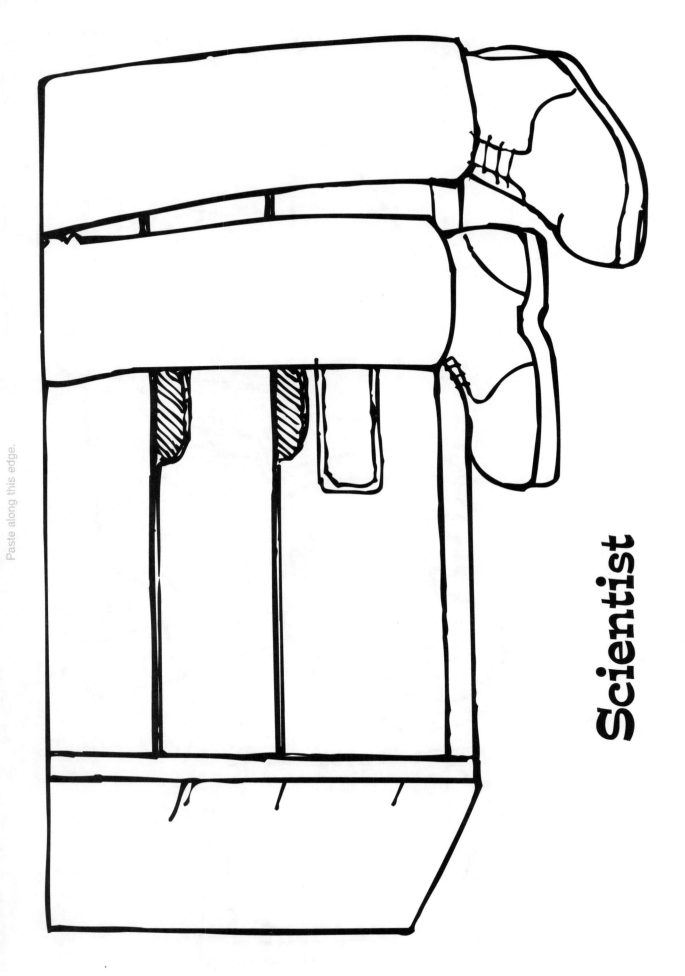

Scientist

Writing Forms • EMC 596

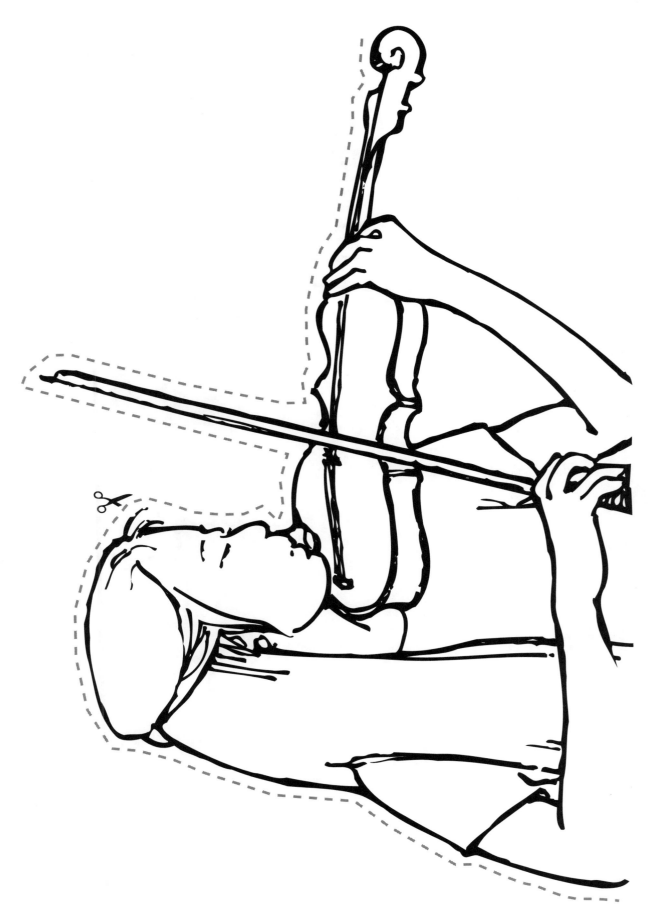

Paste along this edge.

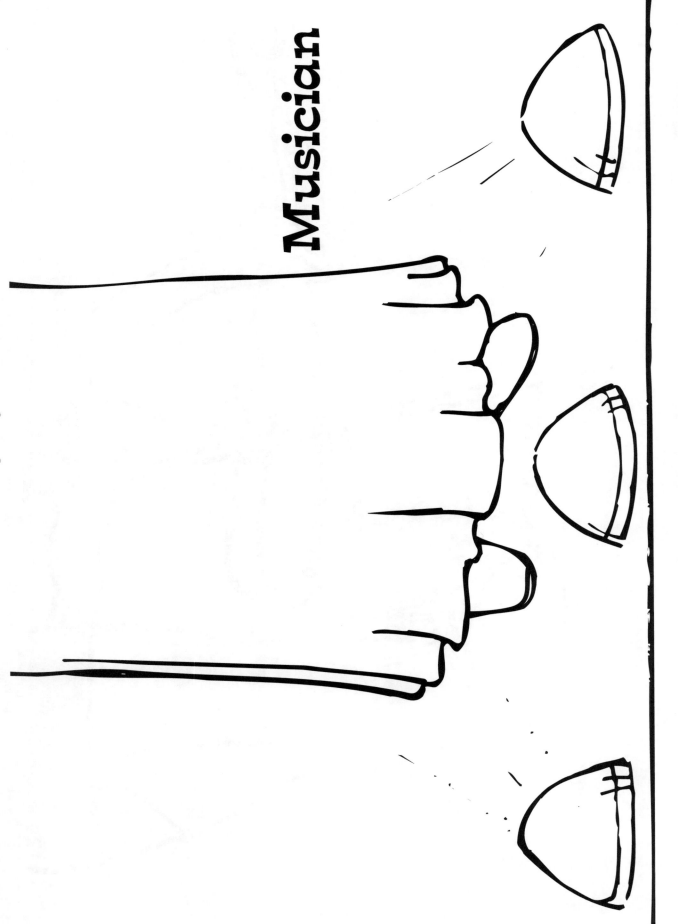

Musician

Writing Forms • EMC 596

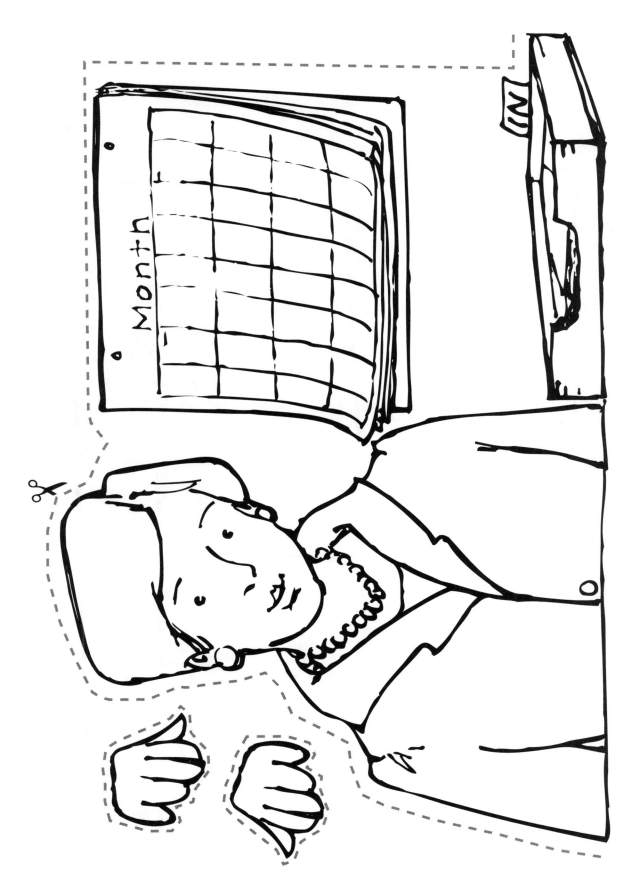

Month

153

Writing Forms • EMC 596

Paste along this edge.

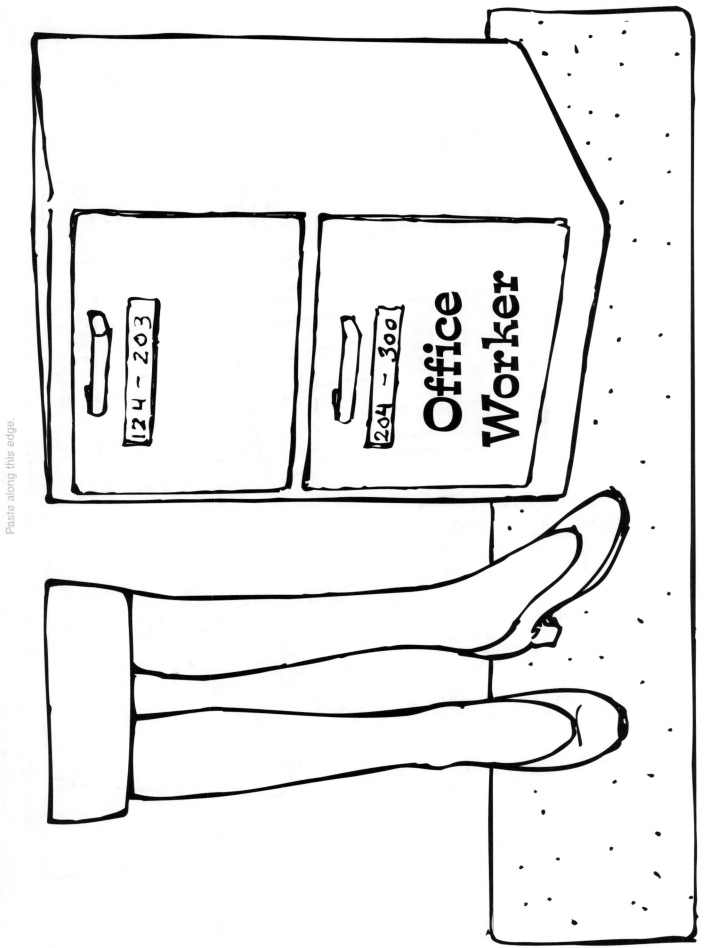

Office Worker

124–203

204–300

Writing Forms • EMC 596

155

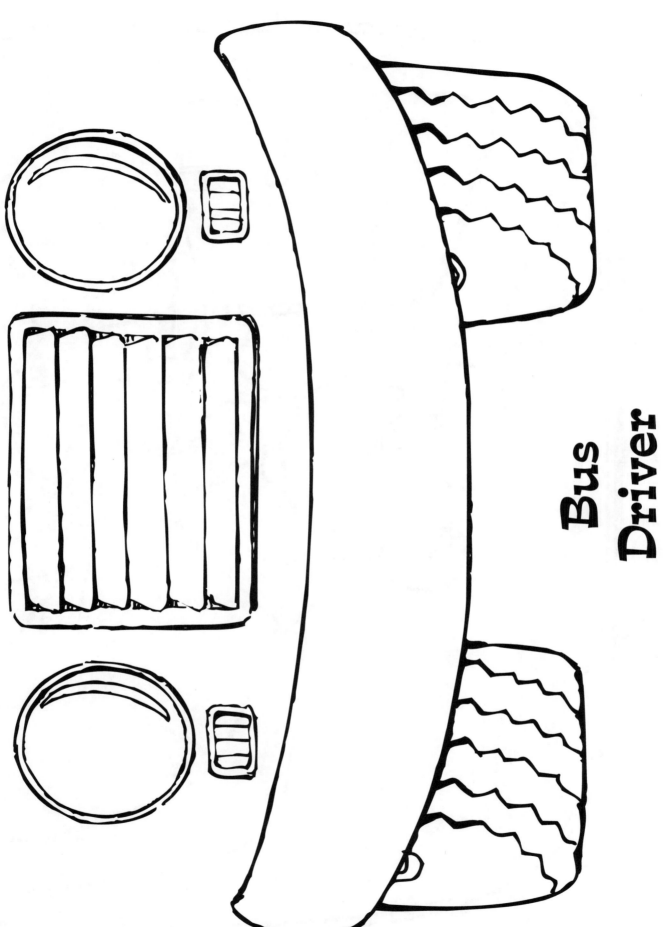

Bus
Driver

Writing Forms • EMC 596

Paste along this edge.

Writing Forms • EMC 596

Paste along this edge.

Dentist

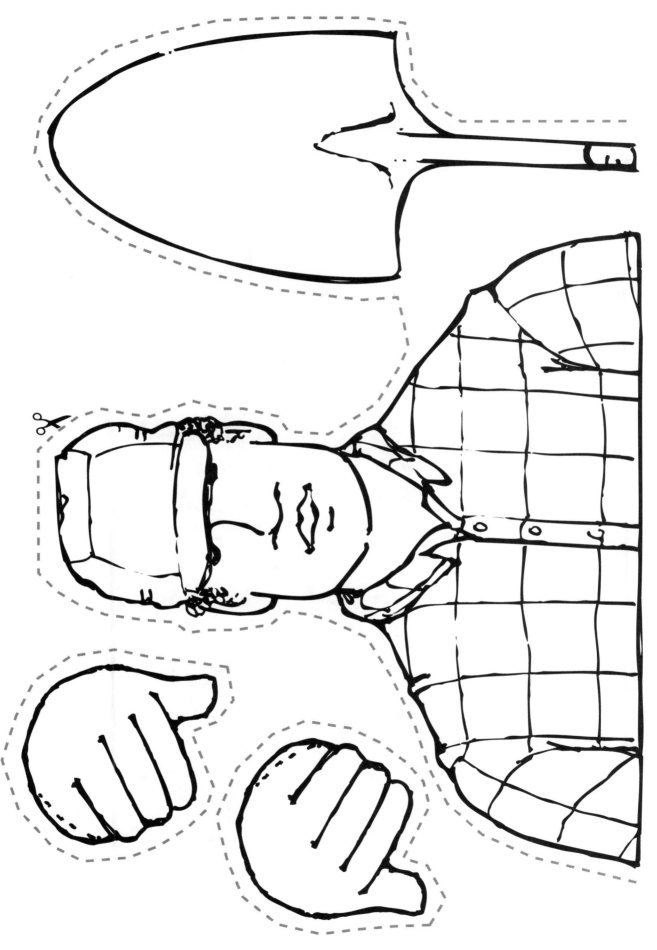

159

Paste along this edge.

Farmer

Writing Forms • EMC 596